Children with Special Needs

A Guide for Parents

RICHARD WOOLFSON

faber and faber

LONDON · BOSTON

First published in 1991
by Faber and Faber Limited
3 Queen Square London WC1N 3AU

Photoset by Parker Typesetting Service Leicester

Printed in England by
Mackays of Chatham PLC, Chatham, Kent

ISBN 0 571 14357 1

5 7 9 10 8 6

CHILDREN WITH SPECIAL NEEDS

Dr Richard Woolfson is a senior educational psychologist, and is an
Associate Fellow of the British Psychological Society. He works for
the Psychological Services in Strathclyde Region, Scotland. He is a
regular contributor to *Nursery World* and *Parents*, writing on child
psychology and education. Richard Woolfson has also written for
The Sunday Times, the *Guardian*, the *Glasgow Herald*, *The Scotsman*,
Baby Magazine, *The Times Educational Supplement*, *Junior Education*
and *Child Education*. He gives regular broadcasts on psychology on
local radio, and has appeared on local and national television. He is
married to an educational psychologist. They have two children.

to Lisa

Contents

Acknowledgements

Thanks to Roger Osborne for his help in preparing the final manuscript; to Tessa and Eve for their love and encouragement; and to Lisa for her love, and for her expert advice on children with special needs.

Introduction

Parents of children with special needs frequently face confusion when they try to understand their child – a confusion that often arises because of their misconception of the child's development. I know a family with two children, the first one developing normally while the second one's development is slow. The mother had no difficulty relating to the younger child when she thought he was simply slow to progress. However, once a specific diagnosis had been made and the mother began to perceive the child as having a particular developmental disorder, she had immense difficulty relating to him. Previously confident in dealing with a child she regarded as normal but a little slow, she was now uncertain how to deal with him.

In this book, the similarities between children with special needs and children whose development is normal are emphasized. Children with special needs have particular weaknesses and make particular demands on their parents that other children do not. But the psychological similarities between all children are usually more important than any differences.

A child with special needs and his parents are much better off nowadays than their counterparts were twenty or even ten years ago. Educational establishments, health services and psychological services have a better understanding of the child's changing needs as he grows older, and can provide better support for parents. Everyone in the family benefits from that. But in some ways, the pressures on parents are greater. Contemporary society expects children with special needs to be more independent than ever before, to be able to do more for themselves. These higher standards can be hard to achieve, and parents can feel tremendous pressure to push their child further than they would like to.

'NEEDS' NOT 'LABELS'

Children with special needs have atypical development. Until this decade, psychologists and child care professionals labelled such children as 'handicapped' or 'subnormal'. So a child paralysed from the waist down, or with weak muscles, or requiring crutches to move around, was labelled 'physically handicapped'; a child who was completely blind, or who had limited vision in both eyes, or who had cataracts, was labelled 'visually handicapped'; and a child unable to keep up with his school work, or suffering from Down's Syndrome, or who failed to learn to speak, or who never developed enough to be able to sit up unsupported, was labelled 'mentally handicapped' or 'mentally subnormal'.

This form of labelling is no longer used. Children with developmental problems are now described as having 'special needs'. This change in terminology is not simply the substitution of one label for another. It occurred for a number of reasons. First, labelling a child 'handicapped' or 'subnormal' does not reveal anything about his strengths, only his weaknesses. It indicates that he has something wrong with him, but not the practical effect of the difficulty. A child may be unable to walk, yet may be confident and determined, able to use elbow crutches to move around the room. Labelling this child 'physically handicapped' focuses on his physical difficulty only, and tells nothing of how he is coping with that difficulty.

Second, the old labels are too general, and fail to recognize essential differences between children. The labels suggest that all 'handicapped' or 'subnormal' children are the same, and need the same sort of help. Yet that is not the case. One child may be independent, and able to talk in simple sentences, but have serious difficulty acquiring basic literacy and numeracy. Another child of the same age may be unable to feed and toilet himself, and only be able to speak using single syllables. Labelling both these children as 'mentally handicapped' or 'mentally subnormal' fails to differentiate the individual level of development in each child.

Third, the terms 'handicapped' and 'subnormal' suggest that the difficulties are all-or-none, that a child is either handicapped or not. But there is no such clear-cut division. Child development occurs on a continuum from normality to abnormality, and all children lie at a point between these two extremes. Children with special needs therefore share many common features with all children. A child with special needs is simply at a different point in the same developmental continuum.

Fourth, the previous terminology does not indicate what sort of measures would help the child overcome, or at least cope with, his developmental difficulty. They only state that he has a problem. Two children may be 'visually handicapped', but one may have no vision at all and need to learn braille, whereas the other may have limited vision and need to read using magnifiers. Labelling both these children 'visually handicapped' fails to say what specific help these children need.

And lastly, labelling a child 'handicapped' or 'subnormal' encourages people to focus on the child's condition, rather than the child himself as an individual. The labels suggest that there is homogeneity amongst children with special needs. That is far from the truth. If you have the opportunity to get to know a child with Down's Syndrome, you will soon realize that the child is a unique individual with his own personality, his own ideas, his own sense of humour and his own level of abilities. He is a child, not a combination of genes. Labelling the child 'Down's Syndrome' is an accurate description of his genetic condition, but it encourages people to view him in stereotyped ways.

This shift in emphasis from handicap (considering the child's weaknesses only) to needs (considering ways in which the child can be supported so that his development is minimally impaired by his difficulty) allows each child to be treated as an individual. It is also more likely to lead to the child receiving appropriate help. In this book, therefore, the term 'special needs' is used in preference to the term 'handicapped'.

The goal of parenthood – no matter the rate of the child's development – is to provide a family environment in which the child can thrive psychologically and physically. There is no one 'right' way to bring up your child with special needs. As you will read in this book, parenthood is about flexibility. There are many principles of child-rearing which apply to all families – and these are explored in the following chapters. But in many cases what suits one set of parents and their child with special needs may not suit another. This book will not provide you with specific answers to your specific questions. It will not tell you what to do every time you have a decision to make about your child. What it will do is provide you with an understanding of your growing child, his emotional and psychological needs, and of how your own skills as parents influence his development.

1·Identifying Special Needs

Parents want their child to develop normally, to acquire the expected skills, and to be like other children of the same age. But although there are similarities among all children (see Appendix I for details of average development at different ages), 'normality' is hard to define because of the very wide range of developmental patterns occurring in young children.

Every child develops at his own rate. For instance, the age at which an infant is able to sit upright by himself, without support, varies from six to nine months. Similarly, the average age at which a child begins to put two words together to form a phrase is around eighteen months, but many toddlers do not reach this stage until twenty-four months, or even older. In most cases these individual differences are normal and are no cause for concern.

And each child may progress at a different rate for each aspect of development. A child may be able to play at a level expected for his age, yet may only be able to talk at a much younger age level. Or he may be as independent as other children of his own age, but be unable to solve jigsaw puzzles which his friends can cope with. These intra-child differences are normal. There is usually cause for concern only when the differences are great, and are present in more than one area of the child's development.

INCIDENCE OF SPECIAL NEEDS

Estimates of the incidence of children with special needs vary considerably. A longitudinal survey of over 2,000 children between the ages of nine and eleven years, living on the Isle of Wight, found that approximately 16 per cent had a difficulty with their development. The National Child Development Study – a long-term project following the progress of all children born in Britain during one particular week in March 1958 – discovered that when the children were seven years old, almost 14 per cent required special help to enable them to cope with the demands of schooling.

In 1978, a major Government commission investigating the education of children with special needs – resulting in the Warnock Report (see Chapter 14) – concluded that approximately one child in five requires some form of special educational provision at some time during their schooling. This 'one in five' figure is generally accepted by professionals as accurately reflecting the number of children who have special needs.

EARLY DISCOVERY AND IDENTIFICATION

The discovery and identification of a child's special needs can take place at different stages during the pre-school years. Severe developmental problems, such as spina bifida or Down's Syndrome, are usually discovered at birth, or within the early weeks of the baby's life. But some difficulties which have a profound effect on a child's development may not be detected until the child is two or three years old, simply because the professionals do not know what to look for. Mosaic Down's Syndrome, for instance, is a rare form of the standard condition, and results in less obvious physical signs. Parents of these children often report that their requests for specialist assessment were originally turned down, despite the apparent developmental difficulties, because their child looked normal.

Health visitors play a key role in monitoring a child's progress, either through regular visits to the family's home, or by developmental check-ups at the local child health clinic. Less severe special needs may not emerge until the child begins to interact with others his own age, whether at mother-and-toddler group, playgroup or nursery. Nursery staff are often the first people to become worried about a child's progress.

It is ironic that while some parents strongly resist the idea that their child has special needs, and consequently reject professional opinions put to them, a number of parents have worries about their child's development yet are unable to find anyone who takes them seriously.

In 1976, a project looked at the experiences of parents with young children with special needs. The researchers found that even when parents were adamant there was something wrong with their child, their views were often ignored by child health professionals. A recent survey on hearing loss in children showed that in three cases out of four, the difficulty was first suspected by the child's parents, whereas only one case in twenty was first suspected by a doctor. And over half of all family doctors consulted by parents of children who were later found to be deaf did not agree the child was deaf. A third of these doctors refused referral to a specialist, although once the child reaches a specialist, far fewer omissions are made.

The last decade has seen an increasing awareness of the importance of stimulation during the pre-school years for children with special needs. More and more educational programmes for this age group are being devised all the time, each aimed at realizing the child's full potential in this very formative period of life. Adequate stimulation in the early years is crucial to the child's later development.

But a 1987 study of paediatricians' attitudes towards children suspected of having special needs confirmed that many professionals are reluctant to refer the child on for specialist developmental assessment. Of the 800 paediatricians involved, a substantial number admitted they did not seek specialist help for a child with mild developmental problems, unless that child had additional emotional or behaviour difficulties. The wait-and-see attitude seems to prevail. This is not because these medical practitioners fail to recognize the importance of the early childhood years – 89 per cent supported intervention before a child reaches the age of seven years, 61 per cent expected a pre-school intervention programme would improve the child's learning ability, and 84 per cent thought it would improve the parents' ability to cope.

There are three main factors underlying this professional

reluctance to formally recognize mild or moderate developmental difficulties. First there is the fear of creating fixed expectations based on a commonly held stereotypic view of children with special needs.

R. K. Merton was the first psychologist to put forward the idea of the self-fulfilling prophecy – the idea that if a person has specific expectations of us then we will behave in ways to confirm that expectation. In other words, the self-fulfilling prophecy becomes true simply because it has been made.

A startling demonstration of this was given by a group of researchers who looked into the effects of teachers' expectations on pupil progress. These researchers looked at 650 pupils between the ages of five and ten years. The pupils' teachers were told that the children had all been assessed intellectually and that they had been divided into three groups. The first group of children was expected to achieve the most educationally, the second group was expected to have average attainments, and the third group was expected to make minimal academic progress during the school year. The teachers were told which pupils in their class fell into each group. In fact, the researchers had randomly allocated the children to each group, although the teachers did not know that. By measuring the pupils' progress at the end of the school year, the researchers would be able to determine the effect, if any, of the self-fulfilling prophecy. Under normal conditions all three groups would make similar progress.

The results showed that the first group (identified to the teachers as the top group) had the highest educational achievements of all, the second group (identified as the average group) had lower achievements educationally, and the third group (identified as the poorest group) made the smallest amount of educational progress.

Clearly this does not mean that if parents have certain expectations of their child then he will always meet them. Raising children is not as easy as that. But it does suggest that higher expectations of a child are more likely to lead to his success than are lower expectations. Some child care professionals argue that by not giving parents a label for their child, low expectations can be avoided.

This line of reasoning is given further support by controversial medical research which has used reconstructive facial surgery to make Down's Syndrome children look less physically distinctive – by reducing tongue size, altering the eyelids and restructuring parts of the nose – in the hope that this might result in an all-round improvement in their development. The researchers postulated that this would stop people classifying them so easily, and consequently prevent them from forming such low expectations of these children. Results have been encouraging. Children who have undergone this surgery function better and more independently in society.

A second reason for the medical profession's reluctance to refer a child for specialist psychological assessment is the fear of upsetting parents unnecessarily. Many parents do find the assessment process an emotional strain, and therefore doctors may prefer to take no action unless there is certainty about the eventual diagnosis. But this benign paternalism (motivated by a genuine desire to protect parents from distress) does not always produce the desired effect. After all, parents may still be worried about their child. And that worry can increase out of all proportion simply because the parents become convinced there is a very deep problem which no one but themselves understands.

Of course, in many cases, developmental assessment reveals that there is nothing wrong with the child's rate of progress, that in fact he is developing normally. The positive use of assessment in that situation is to reassure the child's parents that all is well. Every psychologist would prefer to interview anxious parents and their child rather than to have them sit at home worrying about his progress. Even when the assessment confirms progress is satisfactory, parents usually learn a lot about their child.

And lastly, some doctors hesitate to acknowledge a child's developmental difficulties because of the knowledge that many apparent problems disappear as the child gets older. Children do go through phases in which their development is temporarily arrested. A child may, for instance, use less language at some stage simply because he is going through a phase of shyness; or he may have poor motor coordination when he starts primary schooling, simply because he has had insufficient experience of outdoor play equipment. Psychological intervention for that type of difficulty would be unnecessary.

SIGNIFICANT DIFFERENCES

Some differences in rates of development are worrying. Sometimes the gap in levels of development between a child and other children of his age does indicate a deeper problem. For instance, most children gain bladder control by the time they reach the age of three years, and so parents are justified in seeking professional help if they find their child is still not toilet-trained during the day by the time he is five. However, slow development in only one area rarely indicates a severe problem. A child with a significant developmental difficulty is usually slow in more than one area. In most instances, there needs to be a combination of several delayed features before more substantial investigation is warranted.

The significance of delay in developmental progress is not always clear-cut. Consider the following two children, both aged nineteen months.

Peter: He cannot walk yet, and most people would expect a child to be walking independently before that time. Closer investigation reveals that he appears to be thriving in all other respects. He has started to put two words together to make phrases, he is a very active and alert child, he takes an interest in all that goes on around him, and he tries very hard to pull himself up on to his own two feet using the coffee-table as a prop. Peter sees other children at his mother-and-toddler group who can walk, and he desperately wants to copy them.

James: Like Peter, he cannot walk yet either, and is unable to move himself round a room. Closer investigation reveals that other areas of the boy's progress are also impaired. James makes very few sounds, and those that he does make are unintelligible. His concentration is extremely poor; he will not settle at anything for more than a few seconds. Toys slip out of his hands very easily, as if he does not have adequate control over any of his finger movements. James makes no attempt to walk or pull himself up. He sits about all day, passively, making no attempt to shift his position.

Both these children are lagging behind in their expected rate of physical development. Do you think the lag in development is significant for both these children? Do you think it is too early to say? Do you think one child has a more serious developmental problem than the other? By looking at the children's overall development, it is clear that although ostensibly both have the same rate of physical development, there are vast differences between them. Peter is progressing well, and is showing all the signs of wanting to be mobile. He will be able to walk very soon. James's development shows all-round delay. His slowness in walking is only one of several worrying aspects of his development.

Whether your fears have any foundation in reality or not, you should ask to have your child's development assessed by a suitably qualified psychologist, someone who will look closely at his development. The chances are high that you will receive a sympathetic response from your health visitor or general practitioner when you voice your fears. However, if you are told to stop worrying – or if you anticipate that you will be told to stop worrying – the following suggestions may be helpful:

- *Be prepared to stand your ground.* Don't shy away because someone disagrees with your perceptions of your child. You are the person who spends the most amount of time with him, so you know him better than anyone else.
- *Make a list of all the points that are worrying you, and take this list with you to the interview.* It is very easy in the excitement and anxiety of a clinic interview to forget some of the things you wanted to say. Write these points down in advance, refer to this list during the interview, and try to give specific examples of what is worrying you about your child's development.
- *Ask for the reasons underlying the view that there is nothing wrong with your child.* Look for something more than the predictable clichés 'You know you're such a worrier', 'Lots of children are slow to develop' or 'I'm sure he'll grow out of it'. A decision not to seek specialist help should be made on solid diagnostic grounds, and you should be told what these specific reasons are.
- *Request a second opinion.* Nobody wants to act in a way that might

cause unpleasantness in a doctor–patient relationship. But if you do not get a reasonable and thorough response from your health visitor or general practitioner, ask to see someone else.

AN ACCURATE ASSESSMENT

Once your child is referred for psychological assessment, the psychologist will try to establish an all-round profile of your child's development. Bear in mind, though, psychological measurement is not straightforward. An assessment is like a snapshot. And the psychologist assessing the child must be sure that the snapshot gives him a true picture of the child, that it does not catch him in an untypical posture. Consider the following case:

Danny is four years old. At home he is very outgoing. He takes an interest in all that goes on around him, and he talks fluently. Danny is an active child who enjoys playing with a wide variety of toys. However, outside the family home Danny seems shy, afraid of new situations. When he is faced with unfamiliar faces he becomes clinging and uncommunicative. At his four-year developmental assessment, Danny was overawed by the strange surroundings. Due to this shyness, he acted immaturely and was unenthusiastic about everything he was shown. He would not perform any of the tasks that children of his age are usually capable of completing.

The conclusion reached on the basis of that assessment was that Danny was not progressing as well as he should be. But his parents knew he was a completely different child at home. Are the parents right in thinking that he performed badly because he was shy of his surroundings, or is the professional right in thinking Danny has difficulties?

It is unreasonable to expect a child to give of his best at an assessment when the family have been given an appointment at a clinic on the other side of the city from where they live, when they have had to travel for a couple of hours perhaps taking two buses, followed by a long wait until their name is called by the receptionist. Children give a false impression in these circumstances – and the parents may have lost all patience as well. Accurate assessment of a pre-school child has to be done in a familiar environment in which the child feels comfortable. And the only place that can provide that is home. Clinic-based assessment may be convenient because it saves the professional's time, but in the long run it is unrewarding.

Another important part of your child's assessment is the information you can provide, based on your detailed knowledge of his everyday behaviour. Answer any questions about your child honestly and realistically, and make sure you describe the sorts of toys your child plays with at home, what he is best at, and how much help and encouragement he needs from you. That helps build up your child's developmental profile.

Equally importantly, an accurate assessment will not look at a child's strengths and weaknesses in isolation from his background. A child at the age of five may be expected to be able to cut with scissors. But if he has never had the opportunity to hold a pair of scissors ever before, then of course he will not have mastered that skill yet. That is why a psychologist will always consider details of a child's upbringing when evaluating his progress. Only when all the available information about a child is put together can valid conclusions be reached.

WHY ASSESS AT ALL?

Assessment for its own sake is pointless. For psychologists, developmental assessment is used to identify a child's strengths and weaknesses, in order that areas of difficulty or delay can be targeted for some form of help. Fortunately, there is a wide range of help that can be given to children with developmental difficulties, though much depends on the individual needs of the child and also on the professional services available locally.

Help for young children includes the following:

- *Home teaching.* This aims to encourage specific aspects of the child's development, such as language and communication skills, or visual motor coordination may be appropriate. The home teacher usually visits the child and his parents at home once a week or once a fortnight, for about an hour. In between visits, she will leave toys and activities for the parents to use with their child.

- *Admission to a local nursery*. In many cases, a child's developmental problem can be eased through his mixing with other children of his own age. Nursery placement has this advantage as well as providing the child with individual help should this be required.

- *Admission to a specialist nursery*. Some children have a significant difficulty which prevents them from being able to benefit from attending their local nursery. A special nursery has more staff, who are specially trained, and fewer children. This allows each child in the special nursery to have as much individual attention as is necessary.

- *Physiotherapy*. This encourages a child's physical progress. Physiotherapists will work with a child, usually once a week, at a clinic, in a hospital, in a special school, or in the child's home.

- *Speech therapy*. This service aims to encourage a child's language development. Speech therapists usually work in a clinic or a school. Sessions are usually once weekly, lasting about thirty minutes.

CHECKLISTS OF DEVELOPMENT

Psychologists, paediatricians and other child care professionals have devised many different sets of measuring scales for assessing progress in childhood, for example, the Children's Developmental Progress Charts. Some scales, such as the Bailey Scales of Infant Development, can only be administered by qualified psychologists. The compilers of the Griffiths Mental Development Scales even require that experienced child psychologists and paediatricians undergo further specialized training before being allowed to use the scales. These checklists are normative – they indicate what a child should be able to do at each age – and offer a basic yardstick against which an individual child's progress can be measured. In that way, a child's special needs can be identified.

Despite apparent differences, developmental scales tend to have considerable overlap. The main feature that distinguishes them is the areas of development on which they place most emphasis. Some emphasize the child's physical development, some emphasize social and emotional development, and some emphasize intellectual development. The development checklist given in Appendix I – like some of the other checklists mentioned – focuses on five key areas of child development:

- *gross motor development.* This is the set of physical skills which the child acquires as he grows older. It includes the extent to which the child can coordinate his limbs, the extent to which he can move his body in a controlled way, and the extent to which he has good balance.
- *visual motor development.* This is the ability to coordinate eye and hand movements, and includes the extent to which a child can pick up and hold small objects, use hand implements and control a pencil when drawing or writing.
- *language development.* This is not just the rate at which a child acquires an extensive vocabulary of words. There is receptive language (the degree to which a child can understand what is being said to him) and expressive language (the degree to which he can use language to express his feelings and wishes). In virtually all children, receptive language proceeds at a faster rate than expressive language – normally a child can understand more than he can say.
- *social and emotional development.* This is the child's ability to interact with other children and adults. It also includes the level of the child's independence in basic self-care tasks, such as feeding, dressing and toilet-training.
- *intellectual development.* The best definition of intelligence is that it is the ability that allows a child to make sense of what is going on around him, the ability to adapt to, and cope with, new experiences, and the ability to solve new problems.

Remember that although each of these categories in the developmental checklist is presented independently of the others, areas of development interact. For instance, a child with limited language ability will experience difficulties when trying to relate to other children because he cannot communicate with them. This in turn might affect his gross motor development because he may not have many opportunities to play energetic games with other children.

Similarly, an infant who is unable to sit up on his own will have difficulty in reaching for his toys, which in turn can affect his intellectual development because he is unable to explore his environment adequately.

2 · Coping

A new baby – especially when it is the first child in the family – may represent a daunting prospect for the parents, who may be worried about their own ability to cope with its demands. These worries are naturally heightened in parents of children with developmental difficulties.

'Coping' is a term used to describe a wide range of human responses for managing crises. Psychologists Lazarus and Folman – investigators into the effects of stress – recently defined 'coping' as the constantly changing thoughts and actions by an individual trying to manage a particular external pressure, which he perceives as threatening.

According to this definition, coping has two aspects. First, problem-focused coping: this is the person's attempt to control or alter the event producing stress (for example, coping with a large bank overdraft by trying to earn more money). And second, emotion-focused coping; this is the person's attempt to control the emotions which arise from experiencing the crisis (for example, coping with the anxiety of having a large bank overdraft by reassuring oneself that lots of people have a large overdraft and so it can't be that bad). Both these dimensions should be taken into account when assessing the degree to which a person is coping with trauma.

Problem-focused coping for families with a child who has special needs will include actions which tackle the child's difficulties (for example, encouraging a child with a physical difficulty to increase her ability to walk); and emotion-focused coping will include actions which reduce anxieties and promote the child's positive qualities (for example, taking pleasure in the child's achievements, however slight they may be, instead of worrying about the tasks she cannot master).

The term 'coping' refers to the extent to which parents:

- are able to maintain their own physical health and psychological well-being at the same level it was prior to the birth of the child.
- are able to talk openly between themselves, and with their children, about their feelings and attitudes concerning the child with special needs.
- encourage everyone in the family to develop their own independence, irrespective of the individual attention required by the child with special needs.
- can keep conflict amongst themselves and their children at a manageable level.
- have been able to attain an informed knowledge of the condition that affects their child, and, following on from that, the ease with which they could explain it to someone else.
- are able to establish a consistency in the way they manage all their children.
- retain their ability to laugh at some of the antics their child with special needs gets up to.
- accept that their child has developmental difficulties, without denying any aspect of her special needs.
- are confident about being able to take positive action that will encourage their child with special needs to maximize her full potential.
- keep their feelings of self-blame to a minimum.

While the extent to which a family is able to cope with crisis (such as the birth of a child with special needs) partly depends on what happens after the event, some of the foundations for coping are laid down long before the crisis actually occurs. It is possible to predict with some degree of accuracy which families will be more able to cope with trauma and which families will experience greatest difficulty. In particular, families that have met crises before, that have been able to sit down as a group before reaching a consensus decision, and that allow all the family members to express their feelings – both negative and positive – without criticism, are better placed to cope with current crises.

THAT FIRST MOMENT

You will almost certainly have vivid recollections of the first moment when you realized – or were told – that your child's development was unlikely to progress at a normal rate. Few parents forget the intense emotions of that episode. And, unfortunately, many parents report the unsatisfactory way in which the information was transmitted to them.

Psychologists know that in most instances (except where the problems at birth are very severe), accurate predictions about a baby's level of development when she will be eighteen years old, or ten years old, or even five years old, cannot be made with any confidence. This lack of certainty in the child's pre-school years is something you will have to try and live with.

Lack of justification for such crystal-gazing predictions does not always deter professionals from making them. Diagnosis of developmental problems at birth is frequently made by the duty paediatrician in the local maternity hospital. And it is amazing how many parents of a child with special needs are given dogmatic and pessimistic predictions about their child's long-term prospects. Descriptive phrases such as 'like a vegetable', 'will never sit up' and 'will always be totally dependent' are still used today. That form of professional insensitivity only adds to the parents' concerns. Always remember that the younger the child is when the diagnosis is made, then the less confident you should be about any long-term predictions made at that time.

FIRST REACTION

Diagnosis that a child has special needs can occur at various points in the first few years of the child's life. For some parents, the knowledge is made clear to them at the birth, for example, if the baby is unable to breathe properly, or perhaps if she has an obvious physical abnormality. For some parents, there may be an awareness that their new baby has a problem, perhaps because she cannot suck properly during feeding, but the significance of the problem may be unclear at that stage. In those circumstances, the parents may have to go through a long period of uncertainty before they obtain a more definite picture. And for some parents, the identification of the child's special needs may not arise until the main milestones of development – walking and talking – are not reached long after other children the same age have attained them.

Investigators have found that parental reaction to the diagnosis of developmental difficulties is less negative when the diagnosis is made while the baby is very young and when the child's impairment is less severe. Negative reactions appear stronger when it is the first-born child in the family who has special needs. This probably occurs because the parents have not yet established confidence in their own skills as child-carers. Parents who already have other children, however, have an existing foundation of knowledge and experience of child development, and this gives them a head start in coping with their child who has special needs.

Each parent reacts individually to the realization that their child has special needs which are going to make a significant impact on her life. Despite these individual variations, however, there are a number of typical emotions experienced by many parents in the first couple of hours, days or weeks after the diagnosis. Shock is a common reaction. This can take effect in many different ways, including bursting into tears, and being unable to speak coherently. Some people who experience shock appear extremely calm outwardly, despite their inner turmoil; they may unconsciously 'switch off' from what is being said to them. Other people react to shock by being unable to continue with routine daily tasks at home and work. In many instances, people suffering from shock do not actually realize the impact it is having on them.

Some parents react by denial. People frequently deal with trauma in the first instance by denying that it is happening ('It can't be happening to me', 'The doctors must be confusing my baby with another one'). This is a normal human response to distressing news, and an involuntary psychological mechanism of self-protection. One parent might deny the event outright, accusing the doctors of having made a bad mistake in their diagnosis. Another parent might ask for a different medical opinion because she is sure the first doctor is not very competent. The frequency of denial was confirmed by a recent survey which found that less than 50 per cent of parents with a child who has special needs admitted to the full extent of their child's difficulty.

There may be feelings of anger and blame as a reaction to the news that the child has special needs. The parents may immediately look for someone – or something – to blame for their child's difficulties. These emotions might be focused on themselves ('I didn't take enough care of myself while I was pregnant', 'Perhaps the problem is genetic') or on other people ('The doctors did something wrong during the delivery'). Anger and blame, like denial, are normal human responses to upsetting events.

Guilt is related to feelings of self-blame. Guilt need not be logical, is very unproductive, and can be a self-perpetuating emotion which manifests itself in a variety of ways. ('We must be very bad people for our innocent child to be punished in this way', 'What a terrible burden we've placed on our other children'). Some parents report that their first reaction to the diagnosis was that they wished their child would die. But this then made them feel even more guilty for having had such thoughts at all. It is difficult for parents to admit to themselves that they are having such unacceptable thoughts.

Another common reaction is grief. Parents sometimes react to the diagnosis that their child has special needs by grieving for her, as though she was dead. The child that the parents visualized before the birth has, in a sense, died. In her place is a child with impairments. Some parents require a long time before they can work through this feeling of loss, until they fully accept their child as she really is. One psychological investigation found that over 90 per cent of parents of children with Down's Syndrome still experienced feelings of grief some six years after the birth.

And feelings of hopelessness and despair can be overwhelming ('I just can't face the prospect of raising this child'). The thought that this is a permanent fact of future life can make parents extremely sad and despondent. Like many of the other first reactions, despair generates more despair, creating an ever-increasing spiral of depression and sadness.

Of course, there are many parents who do not experience these emotions. In fact, there are those who claim they have viewed the situation positively right from the start. If you fall into that category, then you are fortunate. It is much more likely, however, that you found yourself in a state of confusion and distress following the diagnosis of your child's developmental difficulty.

Being honest with yourself about your emotions will help you through this stage. It is not pleasant to know that you feel angry, or guilty, or overwhelmed. But these are normal reactions, which you should not try to conceal completely. You may not want all your friends and family to know the full extent of your turmoil – yet you should not pretend to yourself that such inner turmoil does not exist. There is no shame in feeling guilt or embarrassment at having a child with special needs. And accept your own limitations. Maybe you are not the most perfect parent in the world, and maybe you think your neighbour would handle the situation better than you. But that really does not matter. Try to accept your own weaknesses as well as your strengths, so that you avoid becoming excessively self-critical.

Gathering information about your child's condition is another useful strategy. Ignorance of your child's difficulty – including its origin, severity and outlook for the future – creates a breeding ground for fear, uncertainty and confusion. Go back to the professionals who made your child's diagnosis, and ask them to explain everything once again. And ask for advice in areas of uncertainty: there will be a hundred and one things that you find challenging in the initial weeks and months of your baby's life. Don't feel you are being a nuisance by doing this – after all, that is what these professionals are paid for. You have as much right to their time as anyone else. Ask questions, and keep asking them until you feel satisfied with the answer. Some parents prefer to write their questions down before the meeting so that they do not forget anything. Another source of information is the wide range of voluntary organizations concerned with specific developmental problems (see the list of addresses given in Appendix III). Most of these societies have an advice and counselling service, usually run by parents who have experienced your situation. Listening to advice does not mean you will lose control over the management of your baby.

Many parents find that getting involved immediately in the care of their baby – with the washing, feeding and changing – helps tremendously. Although you might want to retire temporarily into a state of shock and despair, do not let that phase persist for long. The more you are involved in the basic care of your child, then the more you will feel that you have some control over her progress. Sympathetic relatives may offer to look after your baby until you fully recover from the birth experience, but while this help is well-intentioned, in the very early days it may actually increase the emotional distance between yourself and your child.

Good communication with your partner is vital. Sharing your concerns with someone else is a positive way of gaining a deeper understanding of your own emotions. It does not have to involve professional counselling, although some people prefer that facility. Candid discussion with your partner will help relieve your feelings of tension. The stiff-upper-lip approach to crisis is rarely effective in helping people come to terms with their own emotions. Similarly, you should try to be honest with your other children. Depending on their age, they may be just as worried as you are. You may be tempted to think that you have enough to worry you just now, without having to handle the questions that your other children want to ask. Yet they have a right to know what is going on. The more they are kept in the dark about what is wrong with the new arrival in the family, the more concerned they are likely to become. And explaining your baby's difficulties to your other children will help clarify your own thoughts.

It is natural that you should want clear-cut predictions to be made about your child. But, as we have already seen, long-term predictions are very unreliable, except in instances of severe impairment. But living with uncertainty is not easy, especially when it concerns your child, and this can add to your frustrations. Many parents say that they never get used to this, and that it is a constant source of stress. Yet if you force professionals into making assertions that cannot really be substantiated then you may be presenting yourself with unnecessary problems.

Another useful technique for helping you cope with those first moments is to remind yourself that although your baby has special needs, she still has the everyday needs of other babies. That your baby has cerebral palsy does not stop her need to be loved, her need to be held closely by you. That your baby has spina bifida does not stop her need to be stimulated and played with. Having special needs does not prevent your child from needing the everyday love, care and attention that all children of her age need.

And lastly, do not automatically assume that each day will always be easier than the one before. Your moods will fluctuate from day to day, in the same way that they did before your child with special needs was born. Yesterday you may have felt very pleased with yourself because you played happily with your baby, without feeling depressed. Today, though, you may become upset at a remark someone makes to you about your child. That is part of family life with a child who has special needs.

TOWARDS COPING

Professionals agree that parents can never truly describe themselves as 'coping' until they genuinely accept the reality of their child's condition, until they have come to terms with the fact that their child has long-term special needs that have to be met. Most families do adapt in this way, although the process is rarely easy.

Observation of families with a child who has special needs has led psychologists to identify a number of factors which appear to influence the way the family adapts in the long term to its new circumstances.

Perhaps the most important factor is the extent to which the child with special needs is able to attain independence. Part of the stress of caring for the child is the ever-present sense that she is dependent on you, and that she will remain dependent on you for the foreseeable future. Yet, in virtually every instance, a child with special needs is able to increase her independence in some way if sufficient help is given to her from the members of her family (this is discussed in more detail in Chapter 11). The more independent your child becomes, the more you will feel able to adapt and cope with her special needs.

Parents usually adapt to their new situation when they perceive themselves as being able to offer their child more than basic care. Washing, feeding and changing are central to the development of a young child, whatever her strengths and weaknesses. But eventually, parental involvement goes beyond these very primary measures, towards more sophisticated involvement (such as playing with her, singing songs and rhymes to her, talking to her, helping her take her first few steps, and so on). Most children with special needs will benefit from that type of parental interaction – and that helps the parents adapt as well.

Families are more able to cope when they have a better understanding of the nature of the child's problem. So find out all you can. This will increase your own feeling that you are in control, and strengthen your ability to reply to questions that will inevitably be posed by friends and relatives. There are many misconceptions about children with special needs. You may find yourself facing unintentionally hurtful remarks made by other people. The clearer your understanding is, the better equipped you will be to withstand these upsets.

Familiarity with the various future options that may be available for your child is useful. This does not mean you should expect to know what your child will be doing five years from now. Yet knowing what the possibilities are has been found to be a factor that helps some parents accept their child with special needs. Responsibility for obtaining that sort of information rests with you, and with the professionals involved in the care of your child.

Families that make a satisfactory adjustment to having a child with special needs also tend to be those that do not make that child the sole and constant focus of attention. Every child in the family needs to be treated as an individual, to be given parental respect and attention. The child with special needs is more likely to be accepted by her brothers and sisters when they themselves do not feel they have to compete with her for their fair share of their parents' attention (this is discussed in more detail in Chapter 4).

Establishing a return to your previous pattern of social life is also extremely important. If your child has special needs this does not mean that you have to spend every minute of your waking time with her. There is no reason why you should not go out for the afternoon or evening, and have your child supervised by a reliable baby-sitter. Breaks from the domestic routine are always refreshing, and a good way of restoring energy and interest.

Some parents obtain great satisfaction from talking with other parents who have children with special needs. That type of forum provides emotional support as well as practical advice. Hearing how other people have coped with circumstances similar to yours may give you ideas on how to cope with the hurdles you are likely to meet. Even if you are the sort of couple who prefer solving problems without outside help, you should still consider this option at some stage.

YOUR CHILD IS A UNIQUE INDIVIDUAL

Getting to know your child as a unique individual – not simply as a child who has a certain condition – is a further factor influencing the adaptation process. In the early days, before you have had time to interact with your baby, your impression of her will be based on the information given to you by other people. It will not be based on your own first-hand experience of meeting her physical and emotional needs. In that sense, your knowledge of your baby will be impersonal. As time goes on, however, you will get to know your child's individual characteristics which differentiate her from other children. And that only serves to increase your confidence in your own parenting skills.

3 · Love and Affection

Emotional bonding between you and your child – the two-way affectionate attachment that develops between you – is the greatest influence on your child's subsequent psychological development. It is the quality of that parent–child relationship which determines many of the child's emotional characteristics in later life.

An emotional attachment between mother and child rarely takes place instantly, even under ideal conditions. Some mothers do say that they felt 'love at first sight' as soon as they set eyes on their child. And there are some mothers who have had a planned pregnancy, who have experienced a satisfactory labour and delivery, and who have given birth to a healthy baby, and yet seem unable to relate to their new baby. Plenty of parents, however, have mixed emotions when they see their newborn for the first time. Thoughts such as 'Is he healthy?', 'Will we be able to cope?', 'Why doesn't he take his feed properly like the other babies?' and 'Will these forceps marks on his face go away, like the doctor says, or is he just saying that to calm us down?', are common. These feelings are understandable, and in most instances give way to more positive feelings as mother and baby get to know each other.

Every parent has an idealized view of their newborn baby, both in terms of physical appearance and personality characteristics. The less the baby actually conforms to that image, the harder it will be for the parents to feel emotionally connected to the baby. This problem becomes more accentuated when the baby has a significant developmental problem, especially when that difficulty is detectable immediately at birth; the bonding process between a mother and her baby with special needs is more vulnerable to disruption and distortion.

VOICE YOUR FEELINGS

Everybody reacts differently to stressful circumstances, and every parent reacts differently to the news that their baby has a developmental difficulty. So the fact that one of your friends reacted stoically in that situation has no bearing on how you should react. Nor does the fact that the parents in last night's television documentary adjusted admirably to meeting the special needs of their baby mean that you should respond in the same way. Your reaction will depend on your personality and past experiences.

Satisfactory emotional bonding between you and your baby, however, is more likely to take place if you are able to accept your own feelings both about yourself and about your baby's condition. The guidelines given in the previous chapter, including being honest with yourself, sharing your feelings with your partner and listening to advice, will help you come to terms with your emotions. There is no advantage to be gained from bottling up your feelings – that won't make them go away. Voicing your feelings is the best strategy.

MYTHS ABOUT BONDING

There are two commonly held views about bonding which are without foundation, and which have been completely disproved by the findings of controlled psychological investigation. Parents can create unnecessary anxiety for themselves if they give credence to these mistaken beliefs.

The first myth is: 'Bonding has to happen before the baby is a few months old or else it will not happen at all'. This myth arises from the process of 'imprinting' found in the animal world. With imprinting, young animals become emotionally attached to any caring adult figure (even to humans in some cases) only during a specific short period at the start of life. If they miss out at that time, they never relate to adult animals later in life.

There is no evidence that humans have a similar critical period. In fact, psychological research has clearly established that emotional connections between parents and their child do not have to be formed during a fixed time-span. With most families, the meshing process between parent and baby takes time, spanning weeks, months and even years. The lack of any critical period is of particular relevance to a baby with special needs, since the formation of emotional attachments in these circumstances may take longer than usual. So parents should not allow themselves to be overwhelmed by feelings of despair because their baby is progressing through his first (or second) year of life and yet they still feel ambivalent towards him. You need time to adjust.

The second inaccurate myth – at one time propounded by psychologists until their own research proved it wrong – is: 'Breast-feeding forges a closer bond between a mother and her baby than bottle-feeding does'. We now know that is nonsense, and the specific method of feeding in itself has little to do with bonding. What matters is the emotional interaction between the mother and her baby, and that interaction can take place through a bottle just as easily as through a breast.

One of the earliest indicators that a child has severe developmental difficulties is his inability to feed properly. Breast-feeding may not be appropriate for a young baby with swallowing difficulties; bottle-feeding, or indeed, tube-feeding, may be the only method of feeding that ensures the child has a regular and sustained intake of food. That need not impair the formation of emotional bonds between parents and child. In any case, there are many women with normal babies who still do not have the luxury of choosing feeding methods – after the birth, they may not produce enough milk or they may be too unwell to feed their baby themselves. And there are some women who simply do not feel comfortable breast-feeding the baby.

What matters is the caring way the parent holds her infant when feeding, and the soothing words she speaks to him. These factors are more important to bonding than whether the milk comes out of a real nipple or a latex one. If an infant is being tube-fed while lying in an incubator, the parents can still have relaxed physical contact with him by touching and stroking him regularly. That the baby is not being breast-fed will, by itself, have no effect on the emotional connection between him and his parents.

PRE-PROGRAMMED FOR BONDING

A newborn baby is already pre-programmed to interact with his parents – he is born with a number of characteristics to enable bonding to take place. A newborn baby's hearing is already tuned to a specific frequency so that he hears human voices in preference to any other sounds in the environment. His vision has the sharpest focus at a point somewhere between 7–9 inches away from his face, which is the distance he's usually held from his parent during feeding. And his voice has a broad range of tones, in order to let his parents know when he is hungry or in distress.

British research psychologist Colin Trevarthan has demonstrated that a young baby also synchronizes his mouth movements with his mother's mouth movements when she talks to him. Close-up video techniques revealed that a baby often pauses when his mother speaks to him, and then makes noises when she stops. Trevarthan calls this interaction *pre-speech* because it is as if the baby is already participating in a conversation. And recent American studies suggest that bonding may even begin in the womb. When a baby's mother read a particular story each day during the last two months of her pregnancy, the baby had a strong positive reaction to that story (compared to his reaction to other stories he had not heard before) when it was read to him three days after he was born. In the light of this evidence, the researchers concluded that the mother–child bond begins even before the infant reaches the outside world.

These predispositions towards bonding confirm that your baby puts as much effort into relating to you, as you do into relating to him. The fact that you may feel low after the birth, or are upset by the realization that your baby has developmental difficulties, will not stop your baby from trying to form an emotional connection with you. Even when a newborn baby has a visual difficulty and cannot focus on his parent's face, he will be able to listen to sounds. Similarly, a baby with a hearing problem will use his vision to relate to you. That is why it is so important to talk to your baby, to play with him and to feed him yourself, in the early stages. Your baby's special difficulties do not reduce his need for that form of stimulation. If anything, that need is heightened.

Where a child has profound developmental difficulties, then many of these predispositions towards bonding may fail to function, and therefore the task of forming an emotional connection with him is more challenging. Yet even in that situation there are actions you can take, because specific features of the mother–child relationship help bonding occur.

Bonding is not simply a matter of the mother meeting the baby's physical needs. Nor does it depend on how much time they spend together, since bonding does not necessarily occur with the adult who spends most time with the child. This is verified by studies of kibbutz children. In these communal establishments, each baby lives with his family at night while during the day he is looked after by a nurse in a nursery, along with all the other kibbutz children. The baby consequently spends most of his waking hours in the care of an adult other than his mother or father. Yet emotional attachments are still formed more often with the mother than with the nurse.

The following guidelines may help you form an attachment between you and your infant:

- *Learn as much as you can about your child's condition.* The more you know about the problem your child faces, the more confident you will feel about managing him. The greater your knowledge, the more likely you are to interpret his behaviour accurately; a mother of a child with cerebral palsy could mistakenly assume the baby's stiff kicking movements represent an attempt to push her away in rejection, when in reality it is simply a muscular reaction. Ignorance of a child's problems may lead to misunderstandings.

- *Persevere in your efforts to soothe your child when he is unhappy.* Bonds appear strongest in families where the mother feels able to calm her baby down when he is distressed. Her self-confidence plays a part too; the mother who has a low opinion of her own skills feels incapable of settling her baby, and this in turn increases his distress, which in turn decreases the mother's self-confidence even more. And so a vicious circle – which is hard to break – can arise. Mothers of babies with special needs often state they have had this type of experience.

- *Give frequent physical contact, of a loving kind, when the baby is fractious and unsettled.* Although physical contact by itself does not guarantee the formation of an attachment, the mother who strokes and cuddles her baby when he is upset is more likely to form an emotional connection with him. Even though you may not know what is upsetting your baby, hold him and cuddle him at these moments.

- *Look for cues from your baby that he wants you to interact with him.* A baby with a developmental problem may not be able to respond to his parents in the normal way. Very elementary features of mother–child interactions – including eye contact, smiling, turn-taking during vocalizations – are not always available to the child with special needs. He may have a visual problem, and not be able to focus on your face. Or he may have a hearing problem, and not be able to respond immediately to your speech. But there will be some cues that he uses in his effort to interact with you. The attachment between you will be enhanced once you are able to identify these cues and to respond to them.

- *Examine your own behaviour when you are with your baby.* The biggest barrier to the formation of bonds between a mother and her baby is tension. A mother who is not relaxed when interacting with her baby will almost certainly convey this to him, which will in turn make him tense, which will increase the mother's own tension, and so on. Tension pushes a mother and her baby apart. So think about the way you react to your baby. Consider how you move towards him when he cries, how you hold him, and the ways you speak to him. If you think you are behaving anxiously, be prepared to modify your actions.

- *Encourage your infant to become independent.* Some parents are tempted to be over-protective with their child who has special needs, on the basis that the infant has enough difficulties without the added strain of having to gain his independence. While that attitude is understandable, this strategy can work against the formation of emotional attachments. Psychologists claim that a child who is denied the opportunity to learn how to cope with basic tasks on his own – such as putting his toys away when he has finished playing with them, or choosing what biscuit he has at tea-time – has greater difficulty bonding with his mother than does a child who is involved in making decisions about what he does.

- *Avoid becoming so caught up in the basic day-to-day management of your baby that you lose sight of what you are doing.* All babies are demanding, both physically and emotionally. But in most instances, the care of a child with special needs at home is even more demanding because he may remain dependent on his parents longer than would normally be expected. One way of coping with these demands is to establish a rigid routine, perhaps by feeding and washing the child at fixed times each day, by doing specific domestic chores according to a pre-arranged schedule, and so on. That can be the easiest method of running an orderly home. And there is no doubt that some form of routine helps a child cope with the world around him. A consistent and well-structured environment can give a child a strong feeling of self-confidence and security. However, don't become too structured in your daily life – you should try to maintain flexibility.

- *Have realistic expectations of yourself and your baby.* You may find that other mothers who were in the maternity hospital at the same time as you have babies that seem alert and curious, whereas the responses your baby makes might seem limited in comparison. But be prepared to interact with your baby at his particular developmental level, even if that level is less advanced than you would have hoped for.

- *Keep playing with your young baby even though he doesn't play with toys the way you would like him to.* Most 'baby' toys are designed for the active enquiring baby who is prepared to reach out and interact with his world. The mobile that hangs down over his cot is expected to attract his interest and encourage his ability to focus and follow objects. Activity centres, with a number of items all making different sights and sounds when touched, are based on the assumption that the baby will stretch his arms out to strike the items. You may feel frustrated if your baby does not behave that way. However, rather than removing these toys in frustration, be prepared to show the infant how to play with them. Show him how the toy makes different sounds, or can be held in different ways. (This is discussed in more detail in Chapter 12.)

Involvement of that nature will bring you and your baby closer together.

MORE THAN ONE PERSON

Your child can form attachments with more than one person, not just with his mother, so he is as likely to form an emotional attachment with his father. In today's society, where fathers take a much more involved part in their infant's care, the chances of bonding between father and baby are high. The previously mentioned guidelines for encouraging bonding are as applicable to fathers as to mothers. (The role of a father within the family is considered in more detail in Chapter 5.)

4 · Brothers and Sisters

Practical circumstances often exert pressure on parents to make the child with special needs the focus of her family. However, the majority of children with special needs have at least one brother or sister, and the danger is that these siblings may get left out.

When a child in the family has special needs, the siblings are more likely to have a mild psychological difficulty. Between 9 and 27 per cent of children with a brother or sister who has special needs exhibit some form of noticeable emotional disturbance. One psychological project found that children with a brother or sister who had spina bifida are four times more likely to experience psychological difficulties, although an investigation into families with a child with Down's Syndrome found that the siblings had a satisfactory level of psychological development.

Where a difficulty emerges, this usually manifests itself in a number of specific ways. In particular, children in a family with a child who has special needs (compared to children in a family where there is no such child) tend to be more antisocial and aggressive towards other members of the family and towards children with whom they interact. Girls seem to be affected more than boys in this way. The children usually have a higher level of anxiety and greater difficulty in coping with everyday life events. In some instances, the child may become withdrawn or even depressed. Children with a brother or sister who has special needs often express the fear that they themselves will develop the same condition. And they may also have lower achievements at school than would be expected.

That does not mean that every child in every family with a child who has special needs is automatically going to be emotionally disadvantaged. Much depends on the individuals involved. In many families, for instance, the other children form a strong attachment to the child with special needs, and they become more caring and altruistic as a result of this. (This is discussed in more detail later in this chapter.) However, findings from psychological research suggest that for many children the psychological advantages of having a brother or sister with special needs are outweighed by the disadvantages, and therefore they require an extra measure of love and sensitivity from their mother and father.

BEING ASKED TO DO MORE

Caring about each other is part of family life. Just as you look after your children and attend to their needs, so should your children gradually develop an attitude of understanding and concern towards people other than themselves. Within sensible limits this form of family responsibility can increase a child's emotional maturity. For instance, expecting a five-year-old child to pour a drink for her brother or sister at the same time that she is pouring a drink for herself is perfectly reasonable. Actions like that encourage her to have a less self-centred perspective on life. And in some cases, doing something for another child in the family can enhance the relationship between the children. A first-born child, for example, often has difficulties in accepting the presence of a new baby in the house. The best way of encouraging the older child to form a close attachment to the baby is to involve her in the practicalities of baby care, whether it is fetching clean nappies out of the cupboard or throwing dirty cotton-wool into the bin. No matter how small the task is, the fact that it involves her in caring for her younger brother or sister makes the child feel important. There are many positive outcomes of giving children an acceptable level of responsibility for others.

But the child who feels her life is taken up by running errands for the rest of her family, or who feels that she is constantly being asked to do more than her friends are asked to do in their families, will react against this. Children with a brother or sister who has special needs often report such feelings. A study into the organization of household responsibilities in families with a child who has either cerebral palsy or spina bifida found that 75 per cent of the other children over seven years of age were expected to help in a large range of basic care activities, including dressing the child who has special needs, helping her with toileting, supervising mealtimes, and generally keeping the child gainfully occupied while the parents were attending to another matter. A similar outcome was found when comparing brothers and sisters of children with impaired hearing.

While involvement with brothers or sisters is not unusual, this level of domestic responsibility is high and may result in the child's resentment. Certainly, if the point is reached where the child complains regularly that she has no time to play with her toys, to watch her television programmes or to be with her friends, then the parents should closely scrutinize the domestic burden on her.

NOBODY CARES FOR ME

You have a limited amount of time to spend with your children, and simple logic dictates that the more children there are in your family then the less time there is available for each individual. Most children, though, learn to adapt to this situation without undue concern. When one of the children has special needs, however, she is likely to demand more of your attention than her brothers and sisters. You will probably be involved in more clinic visits for speech therapy, developmental assessments, and so on, all of which are essential but very time-consuming. And additionally, a child with special needs often has a slower rate of acquiring independence than other children, with the practical implication that she needs help at an age when her brothers and sisters could do things for themselves. Many parents of children with developmental problems openly admit that the family's routine, the family's financial resources and the family's recreational activities all centre around the needs of the child with difficulties. This is not because the parents love the child who has special needs more than the others but because the child simply cannot function without that extra level of individual attention.

But the net effect of this can be that the other children in the family feel neglected, that they come second in the list of family priorities. The other children may not be mature enough to see the situation except from their own point of view. They may feel uncared for, that the mother and father use the child with special needs as an excuse to ignore them because in reality they do not love them. Another common feeling amongst siblings is that only the achievements of the child with special needs matter to the parents, because she will receive positive comments for doing something that went unnoticed when they did it. The child with visual impairment who crosses the room confidently from one side to the other without help will be greeted with encouragement from her parents, whereas the other children completed the same action without any such response. Parents have this differential reaction because what is easy and routine for the siblings may be a monumental challenge for the child with special needs. Although that is logical, it may not make it any easier for the siblings to accept without feelings of resentment.

EXPECTING TOO MUCH

Almost as soon as a couple realize that the woman is pregnant, they begin to form ideas about what they hope the child-to-be will be like, what they hope she will achieve, how they hope she will relate to them and the sorts of standards they hope she will adopt. Through the process of child development within the family, the parents often modify these pre-birth hopes to accommodate the individual strengths and weaknesses of their child. A child with special needs poses a particular problem in this respect since – depending on the child's developmental difficulties – the child may be totally unable to attain standards that remotely resemble the parents' pre-birth ideas. Parents may experience emotional distress coming to terms with that reality.

Without realizing they are doing so, parents may compensate for this by projecting their expectations on to the siblings of the child with special needs so that the expectations of these children are much higher than the normal expectations parents have of their children. This process usually operates at an unconscious level. One research study, investigating families with an epileptic child, found that parents expected their non-affected children to attain unrealistically high scores in educational assignments. Siblings of children with special needs often comment that their childhood was a time of pressure to be somebody that they were not. For instance, they may feel they were expected to come top in their class at school, to be extremely popular with other children, and even to win prizes at sport.

Some siblings of children with special needs become aware very early on in life that they are expected to be 'normal', and that deviance in any form is not tolerated by their parents. The guidelines of normality are very flexible, and no two children follow the developmental path in exactly the same way. However, in these families, parents may construct a very rigid normality, in which the child should be well-behaved at all times, should be helpful and courteous to everyone, should have no personal problems, and so on. This rather idealized view of childhood – born out of the 'you should think yourself lucky you don't have your sister's problem' line of reasoning – denies the non-affected child the right to her individuality. Families need to set standards, parents need to have expectations of their children. But the children will not thrive if these expectations are so rigid that they do not allow the children to develop their own individuality.

DIFFERENCES BETWEEN FAMILIES

Social class – a term popular with researchers but highly controversial – is a relevant factor when considering the impact of a child with special needs on the family. For instance, an investigation found that brothers and sisters of a child with special needs in a working-class family spend a great deal of time worrying about how their parents will cope with the physical demands of caring for the child. In contrast, brothers and sisters in a middle-class family spend more time worrying about the child's limitations. Social class appears to affect the parental reactions to the child who has special needs and this in turn affects the reaction of the other children in the family.

Family size also affects the impact of a child with special needs. Children in smaller families, where there are one or two children altogether, have a higher likelihood of emotional problems than do children in larger families, where there are upward of three other children. This difference occurs even when comparisons are made between families of the same social class. Psychologists have put forward a number of theories to account for this phenomenon. The most convincing one is that the bigger the family, then the more diluted become the demands of the child with special needs. There are simply more helping hands in a large family than in a small family. As well as that, a child with special needs amongst a large group of brothers and sisters is not as obtrusive.

FAMILY CHARACTERISTICS

The way a child reacts to a brother or sister with special needs depends on several factors. First, there is the child's age. A child several years older than the child who has special needs will have been aware of the difficulties right from the beginning, and will have been involved from the moment the child was brought home from the maternity hospital. A child younger than the child with special needs is unlikely to show any real understanding until she reaches school age. By missing out on the early adjustment the family had to make, the younger child's awareness takes longer to develop. Second, there is the sex of the child; girls are more likely to be adversely affected by the presence of a child with special needs in the family than are boys. This is probably due to the fact that girls are usually given more family responsibilities than boys and are therefore more likely to feel the presence of the child with special needs as a burden. Third, there is the severity of the difficulties. The greater the impairment of the child with special needs, then the greater the impact on other children in the family. One study, however, found that there were no emotional difficulties in brothers and sisters of a child with special needs when the child's difficulty was physical rather than intellectual or developmental.

PSYCHOLOGICAL ADVANTAGES

It is certainly not all bad news for the brothers and sisters of a child who has special needs, and it is important that parents do not focus entirely on the negative impact it creates. There are two main psychological benefits accruing to the other children in the family.

First, there is often an increased sense of altruism. When brothers and sisters of a child with special needs reach adulthood, they frequently report themselves to have an increased tolerance of other people, a better ability to accept the strengths and weaknesses of others whom they meet, and a greater interest in humanitarian issues in society. Being brought up in a family where one of the children requires extra help seems to encourage the siblings to develop compassionate characteristics. Second, there may be increased self-esteem. Paradoxically, the presence of a child with special needs in the family can actually reinforce the normality of the other children. In a sense, the presence of that child acts as a constant reminder to everyone else that their own development is progressing normally. Psychologists claim that accounts for such children having an unexpectedly high level of self-confidence.

While not minimizing the detrimental effects that the child with special needs has on the psychological welfare of the brothers and sisters, these positive spin-offs may provide some comfort to parents.

GUIDELINES

If you have a child with special needs in your family, when dealing with your other children:

- *Encourage them to communicate with each other, and you, about the child's abnormalities.* This type of communication amongst children in a family does not often happen spontaneously. Let them talk about the effect their brother or sister has on them personally.
- *Give them information about the nature of the child's difficulty.* Anxiety frequently stems from misunderstanding or lack of knowledge of the condition affecting their brother or sister.
- *Pitch any discussion of special needs at a level the children can understand.* Use terms that are meaningful. Although a child may not grasp the meaning of 'brain damage', she will understand 'unable

to learn to read'. Likewise, a child will grasp the idea of 'unable to run' more easily than she will grasp the idea of 'spinal deformity'. Even limited explanations are better than none at all.

- *Let them express their feelings openly and honestly.* It is not a crime to admit fear at having a brother who is blind, or embarrassment at having a slow-learning sister. Ignoring these worries will not make them go away. A more effective strategy is to let the children come to terms with these feelings, through candid discussion within a caring family environment.
- *Prepare them for the possibility of hurtful remarks from other children.* Explain to your children that others probably don't understand the problems of a child with special needs, and might make insulting comments. Your children's anguish in these situations could be reduced if you have told them that these hurtful remarks stem from ignorance rather than malevolence.
- *Involve them in the care of the child who has special needs.* When the children are allowed to become involved in the day-to-day management of the child with special needs – without being given overwhelming responsibility – their self-esteem improves, as does their pride in their brother's or sister's achievements.

All the children in your family have their own lives to lead, not just the child with special needs. Do not cover up the child's special needs, but do not make them a permanent and all-encompassing focus for the whole family. A balanced perspective lets every child get individual parental love and attention.

5 · Effect on the Family

When the weeks and months immediately following the diagnosis of the child's difficulties have passed, and once the initial reactions have eased, most parents make a conscious effort to 'get things back to normal'. The other children try to resume their former role in the family, just as they did before the birth, and the adults attempt to return to their former domestic routine. The family's ability to readjust in that way is one indication that they are beginning to cope with their new situation.

However, even though parents may cope with the emotional pressures of this early phase, they also have to cope with other pressures that appear later on. Awareness of these long-term stresses on your family may at least help you minimize their impact, and at best help you avoid them altogether.

FAMILY ISOLATION

Many parents of children with special needs report a strong sense of isolation, a sense of enforced detachment from friends, relatives and society. These parents often say that they are made to feel different because other people cannot – or will not – understand the special challenges facing them.

This strong sense of isolation originates from three different sources. First, from the behaviour of the family itself. Caring for a child with special needs usually necessitates a great deal of physical and emotional input from the parents, particularly during the pre-school years. This means that there is less time available for meeting friends, going to the movies, and for participating generally in life outside the family home. Although this applies to most families with a new baby, in normal circumstances a child will achieve independence earlier than a child with special needs.

But not all parents react this way. A research project in the 1970s, focusing on parents of children with special needs, showed that although 30 per cent of the parents reported that their child's condition restricted their social life, nearly 15 per cent reported that their child's difficulties actually improved it. This perceived improvement possibly occurred because these parents made more of an effort to sustain their social life than they would have done in normal circumstances.

Some parents cope by deliberately isolating themselves from their friends. A study in 1977 found that 25 per cent of families with a child who has special needs had consciously chosen to push themselves into complete social isolation, and that they did so to protect themselves from the hurtful comments and questions of other people. In the long term, though, this is not a strategy you should adopt. Remember that eventually your child will have to interact with others outside your family – and if you are not ready to cope with society, you cannot realistically expect your child to do so.

Second, there is also a psychological dimension to isolation, something more than the amount of social contacts a couple has. After all, we have all had the experience of feeling lonely in a crowd – that feeling of being beside others yet at the same time emotionally distant from them. Some couples with a child who has special needs lead a very active social life; they go out with their friends several evenings a week, and are also busy at the weekends. But these couples may still feel isolated. It is the quality of the social contacts which matters.

Also, adults who are naturally shy may find having a child with special needs gives them the long-awaited excuse to withdraw from society, and unconsciously they take advantage of this opportunity. Others may be so embittered by their experience that they want nothing to do with other people. Individual personality characteristics clearly influence the amount of emotional satisfaction obtained from social relationships.

A third source of a family's isolation is other people's attitudes.

Even in today's supposedly enlightened society, many families with a child who has special needs feel they are stigmatized. Adults and children who have no first-hand experience of children with special needs may have difficulty relating to them. You have probably seen instances of someone crossing the road in order to avoid passing by a child in a wheelchair. Perhaps this stems from an irrational fear of the unknown. Perhaps it stems from ignorance. Whatever the underlying reason, the effect is to make the couple feel as if their family has some sort of highly infectious disease. Numerous studies have confirmed the very pervasive nature of this form of social rejection, whether it arises from deliberate ill-will or not.

In 1973, Margaret Woodburn, a psychologist specializing in the study of families with children who have special needs, asked a group of these mothers, 'What comments, reactions or attitudes do you particularly dislike?'. Almost 20 per cent of the sample put 'false sympathy' at the top of their list. Genuine sympathy which reflected the questioner's real concern and compassion was always welcome, while insincere sympathy which barely masked the questioner's curiosity was not. Next on the list of distasteful social comments came 'outspoken advice' ('You should put that child in a residential home where he can be properly looked after'), and this was closely followed by remarks about the child's lack of mobility ('Most children his age are walking steadily by now'). Parents do not find these comments helpful.

Approximately 30 per cent of the mothers in Woodburn's investigation had experienced either verbal aggression ('You're wrong letting him drink out of a bottle at his age') from neighbours, or even from complete strangers who just happened to be passing at the time. They had also experienced uncaring social behaviour (someone walking by a child who has a physical disability, then coming back to stare more closely at him). Many of the mothers reacted angrily to verbal aggression. But even those who did not were still very upset. Some admitted to the investigators that they were more apprehensive about taking their child out in public in future, even though they knew this would only increase the child's sense of isolation. Alas, developing a 'thick skin' is often a necessary part of being a parent of a child with special needs. Giving into society's ignorance only helps perpetuate it.

Another way of combating the family's potential isolation is to join a parent support-group, organized and attended by other parents of children with similar developmental difficulties. This type of group allows parents to share their experiences. Although that in itself will not automatically increase parents' confidence in coping with the reactions of others, it usually helps. The realization that others are experiencing the same stress can have a therapeutic effect. And support-groups also provide up-to-date research information and management advice. Not everyone likes to be part of a group, and you may feel uncomfortable in that situation. But try it anyway – if you don't like it, you don't need to go back.

THE CHILD'S ISOLATION

The child with special needs himself has to cope with the potential hazard of social isolation. One study found that children with special needs had 30 per cent fewer social contacts than did other children their own age. A lot depends on the child's particular difficulty. For instance, children with a mild physical difficulty were found to have a better social life than children with a mild learning difficulty. However, more than 50 per cent of children confined to a wheelchair were found to have no friends at all in their neighbourhood. Severe lack of mobility in childhood has a major limiting effect on social interaction.

The impact of isolation becomes more significant during the teenage years. In 1976, research psychologists Nicola Madge and Meg Fassam interviewed adolescents with special needs about their social experiences. As was expected, the researchers found that these children had a more restricted social life than ordinary children their own age. Those adolescents who felt the least isolated, however, were those integrated into their local school, whereas those who felt most isolated were those who attended a segregated special school. (This is discussed more fully in Chapter 13.)

Isolation can be avoided by ensuring that your child mixes with other children of his own age, in as many different settings as possible, particularly those which involve some form of adult supervision. (This is discussed in more detail in Chapter 12.) Where a child's difficulties are not all-pervasive, he should make use of local play facilities. A boy with learning difficulties, for instance, will be able to cope with the demands of a Cub group. Cub 'badges' vary in difficulty, and a sensitive leader will be able to guide a child with special needs through some of them. Sporting activities, such as swimming, are also good opportunities for children of all abilities to interact.

Your child may not thank you for launching him into new social opportunities. Every child is shy sometimes, and even the most vivacious, talkative child can 'dry up' when he feels overwhelmed by the novelty of an unfamiliar situation. Have realistic expectations of your child's social skills. Although every child matures at a different rate, the following are approximate age guidelines:

- *one week old:* A newborn baby cannot differentiate one person from another, and therefore does not show any signs of shyness. It is true that some babies will only take a feed from one person in particular, and not from anyone else. But apart from that instance, most babies will happily interact with anyone who shows them kindness and interest.

- *six months old:* by this age the infant has begun to differentiate familiar faces from unfamiliar ones. Your child may be able to recognize the people in his immediate family. He will probably be shy of strangers, no longer friendly to anyone and everyone. Your child may not want to leave your knee when there is a stranger close by. Medical examinations at this stage often prove to be trying for all concerned because of this.

- *one year:* the child probably has greater awareness of who is familiar and who is not. He still remains shy, however, and may be very clingy with you when taken into new situations. The child may even cover his eyes with his hands or arms when a stranger approaches. A child of this age taken to a mother-and-toddler group often sits 'glued' to his mother, desperately keen to join in the fun and games yet at the same time not secure enough to leave his mother for an independent foray into the playroom.

- *two years:* at this age a child has a greater degree of self-confidence, yet may still hesitate to relate to people he does not know. A stranger is more likely to be greeted with silence than tears. A child who is able to walk at this age can remove himself physically from any situation he does not like – when he feels shy of anyone he simply runs out of the room.

- *three years:* many children of this age are confident enough to accept attention from children and adults they do not know well – albeit cautiously. The typical three-year-old child is a combination of increased self-assuredness and decreased shyness, which means he is more able to cope with meeting new children and adults. A playgroup is well suited to the social needs of a child this age, and most three-year-olds enjoy playing with other children of their own age.

- *five years:* most of the earlier signs of shyness have gone, partly due to the increased confidence that comes with growing up, and partly due to the experience of social encounters in the earlier years. Even so, the child aged five years may still show some shyness when in a totally new situation.

- *the older child:* from about the age of five years upwards, a child may be able to talk about his shyness, and may be able to express his feelings. This can be helpful for parents trying to understand their shy child because what may appear disconcerting for adults may not be the factor that upsets a child. So ask your older child what it is about the social encounter that makes him uneasy. Your attentiveness to his shyness may encourage him to be more confident the next time.

Despite any natural shyness, however, a child with special needs should be given that extra 'push' to mix with others, and the following strategies may help your child mix better with others:

- *Build up your child's self-confidence.* He may be embarrassed about his problems, whether it is a lack of mobility or poor speech, and have low self-confidence. Discuss his strong points with him, for example, that he is good at singing, or that he is kind. Emphasize these positive attributes, stressing all the time that these features will make other children like him.

- *Give your child lots of social experiences.* You cannot reasonably expect your child to become socially confident unless he has plenty of opportunities to mix with other children. Make sure he plays with children his own age. Invite other children to your house to play with your child, and take him to playgroup or nursery, depending on his age. He needs a variety of social situations in which he can interact with other children.

- *Do not let your child avoid people.* He may prefer to be on his own, and you may be tempted to let that become his way of life. Yet the more you allow him to back away from social encounters, the more entrenched he will become in his isolation.

- *Teach your child opening strategies.* The first few moments in any meeting are the most difficult, and much of the tension eases after that. Your child may find the uncertainty of what to do in these initial seconds is what troubles him most, and therefore you should teach him specific strategies to use when he meets new people. Be quite specific in your advice: for instance, tell your child that he should ask the other child to play a game, or that he should ask the other child about his favourite television programmes, or that he should suggest they play with his colouring books and crayons. The actual opening move itself does not matter. What does matter is that your child has something definite to do in these first few crucial moments.

- *Practise these techniques.* Let your child use these strategies in role-play situations in the comfort and security of his own home. A young child enjoys make-believe games, and will be comfortable 'pretending' to meet people. Your guidance through role-play will help him gain confidence. The role-play situations could be shopping, talking to other children at playgroup or nursery, or answering the telephone. Teach your child how he should react and then act it out, rather as he might rehearse lines from a play. This way he will learn how to cope without experiencing the embarrassment of making mistakes in front of other people in the process.

- *Try to anticipate the behaviour of other children.* Prepare him for the comments he is likely to receive when he ventures out of the house. Explain that everyone is different, that no two people are the same. Emphasize to your child that his difficulties are outweighed by his good qualities. And reiterate that well-worn cliché that other children will stop teasing him once they realize the teasing has no effect. A little advance preparation will help your child deal with the real thing when it arises.

OVER-PROTECTION/OVER-INDULGENCE

Over-protection and over-indulgence of the child with special needs is a common occurrence. Every child is vulnerable in the early stages of life. Right from birth, a new baby relies totally on adults to meet its needs. Without parental help it cannot keep warm during cold nights, and it cannot keep clean. A newborn baby would die without caring attention from adults. And a new baby with developmental difficulties is especially vulnerable – he will remain dependent on parental help for an even longer period.

Although this concept of 'extended dependency' is a logical explanation for parents over-indulging their child with special needs, it does not appear to be the complete picture. Some psychologists point to the existence of parental guilt as the driving force behind over-protectiveness. Parents who in some way feel responsible for their child's difficulties may unconsciously compensate for this by over-indulging him. Fear is another factor. Parents may somehow feel that the child with special needs will be at risk in some way if he is encouraged to tackle new tasks. In addition, some parents enjoy having a baby in the house, and maintaining the child's dependence on them is one way of preserving that status.

You need to look closely at the way you manage your child with special needs. You may react defensively to a friend's suggestion that your child is over-indulged. But try to reach beyond that initial feeling. Ask yourself if your expectations are unnecessarily low, or if he is allowed to get away with more breaches of discipline than your other children. Unless you are genuinely satisfied that the demands you are making on your child are sufficiently high to promote his development, think again. Your expectations of your child with special needs might be a reflection of your attitudes, not of his true potential.

MARITAL STRESS

Professionals have shown considerable interest in the extent of marital dissatisfaction and divorce among families with a child who has special needs – encouragingly, though, the incidence is low. In 1981, a report from the Central Statistics Office confirmed that nearly 90 per cent of all families with a child who has special needs were headed by two parents. This statistic is remarkable when seen against the background of a contemporary society in which approximately one marriage in three ends in divorce.

Some couples report that the presence of a child with developmental difficulties has positively enhanced their marital relationship. The likeliest explanation of this outcome is that the task of caring for the child pulls parents closer together emotionally. This effect becomes stronger when the child's difficulties are more severe.

Comparing families of a child who has special needs with ordinary families, studies have found that the number of years parents have been married before the birth of their child is directly related to marital harmony (couples married for less than five years have more difficulty in coping than couples married more than five years). The quality of the marriage before the birth of the baby affects the parents' future relationship – prior marital difficulties are usually increased by the presence of a child with special needs. Not surprisingly, the greater the child's developmental difficulties (and in particular the more daily activities in which the child is limited), then the greater the strain on the marriage. And fear of future pregnancy can be a source of considerable stress, especially when the child with special needs is the first-born in the family.

Despite these findings, however, families with a child who has special needs are no more likely to experience separation or divorce than are ordinary families. The most significant influence in maintaining the marriage is the couple's emotional stability prior to the birth – in divorced families with a child who has special needs, approximately 75 per cent of the couples have experienced severe marital unhappiness before the birth of their child.

FATHER'S ROLE

The biggest change in the father's role within the family, over the past ten to twenty years, has been the degree to which he is involved in matters of childcare. No longer is the man's role rigidly confined to earning money, to discussing political matters, to making decisions about how the family's income should be spent, or to kissing the children goodnight after they have been fed, washed and changed by their mother. The contemporary father is able to play an active part in every aspect of his child's life – if he wants to.

This change in the father's role runs parallel with changes in the mother's. Whereas in previous decades a woman was forced to give up her career when she had children, many women now have a choice of returning to work while their baby is young – thereby sharing the care of the child with somebody else – or staying at home in the child's pre-school years. Even where the mother does not want to return to work, she will still expect her partner to participate in domestic activities.

The combined effect of these role changes is that caring for the children is more frequently shared between the parents. Psychologists expected this trend to be reflected in families with a child who has special needs. However, this pattern is far from universal, although there has been an overall trend towards greater paternal involvement.

An early study into this dimension of family life compared the perceptions of parents with children with cerebral palsy with the perceptions of a control group of fathers with non-impaired children. This 1970 project found no evidence to support the view that a high proportion of fathers of children with cerebral palsy are more involved with their children than are other fathers.

A more detailed study in 1971 measured the amount of the father's participation in the basic physical care of their child with special needs, when the child was very young. The results indicated that at least 35 per cent of the fathers gave the mother no help at all with bathing the baby, changing his nappies or going shopping. The researchers noted, though, that 21 per cent of the fathers did offer help with one of these three activities, 18 per cent with two of them, and 21 per cent gave the mother support with all three of these tasks.

By 1973 a different picture was beginning to emerge. Margaret Woodburn's study of families with a child who has special needs concluded that the majority of mothers spoke positively of their husband's support, that 35 per cent of the fathers spent 'more than average' time with their child, and that 15 per cent of the fathers spent 'less than average time' with their child. Where the child's developmental difficulties were severe, 10 per cent of the fathers spent even more time with their child. In addition, 60 per cent of the mothers stated that decisions about childcare were shared equally with their partner.

Subsequent studies have reached conflicting conclusions. For instance, one found that fewer than 25 per cent of fathers with a child who has special needs help their wives to any real extent, while in contrast, another noted that 27 per cent of fathers gave up work at some time to care for their child with special needs.

What clearly emerges from all this research is that mothers who are given practical and emotional support by their partner consider this to have a positive effect on their own ability to cope with their child who has special needs. It is important, therefore, that the child's father should be involved right from the start. But too often this does not happen, usually because of practical restraints. For instance, most professionals dealing with young children work regular office hours, and appointments may not tie in with the father's free time – thus he may be excluded from the early stages of the assessment and diagnostic process. Lack of involvement at that stage can have a carry-over effect throughout the child's life. The father's participation in decisions about the child with special needs should be considered by both parents and encouraged by professionals from the earliest possible moments.

SINGLE PARENTS

Some single-parent families do arise from the death of one of the parents, or from the mother never having been married. But the majority of single-parent families arise from separation or divorce.

Becoming a single-parent family is therefore often the end point in a painful process that usually started years before, and is the final stage of a long-term disruption to family relationships. Estimates suggest that between one in seven and one in twelve of all single-parent families have a child with special needs. A survey conducted in 1982 estimated there are 4,600,000 such families in America alone.

Single-parent families face a number of distinct problems not experienced by two-parent families. There is a shortage of time (the single parent has to work to pay bills, and has less time to give to her child), a lack of emotional support (she has to make all the minor and major family decisions herself), poorer housing conditions (often the family home is sold following the separation, and the single-parent family is forced into inferior housing stock) and a reduced income (especially when maintenance payments are irregular). All these factors cause the single mother even more stress when she has to care for the additional demands of a child with special needs.

Many professionals take the view that while quality day care for a child with special needs is a positive way of enhancing his development in the pre-school years, this is particularly true when the child lives in a single-parent family. If you are in this situation, don't hesitate to take advantage of any such facilities offered to your child (for example, day nursery, playgroup). It is in both your interests to utilize this type of pre-school provision.

SCAPEGOATING

A child with special needs can provide a convenient scapegoat for the family. This type of scapegoating occurs when the parents unconsciously use their child to vent their anxieties. Rather than facing up to their own relationship problems, a couple might displace the anger and disappointment they feel towards each other, on to their child.

To identify whether scapegoating is occurring in your family, ask yourself the following questions:

- Do you automatically assume all your troubles are caused by having a child with special needs in the family?

- Do you think your marital relationship was worry-free before your child with special needs was born?
- Do you consider your other children give you more pleasure than your child with special needs?
- Do you frequently think your child with special needs is so demanding that you have no time to be on your own?

If your answer to these questions is 'no', then it is unlikely that you are scapegoating your child with special needs. You probably have a realistic perception of the stresses he is causing you. If the answer to these questions is 'yes', then you may be using your child unfairly as a focus for your concerns – and in that situation you should look closely at all the stresses in your life, in an effort to obtain a more balanced perspective. Talking the matter over with a close friend or relative may help you gain a clearer understanding.

6 · Self-image

Psychologists attribute great importance to 'self-image' because of its impact on personality development. The terms 'self-image', 'self-concept' or 'self-esteem' (all of which refer to the same idea) are defined as a child's sense of being a unique individual, the feelings of personal worth she has, and the way she sees herself in relation to other children and adults.

A good self-image is an essential ingredient of personal happiness and contentment with oneself. Children with a poor self-image find difficulty in giving love to (or receiving love from) other children and adults, including their parents. They also tend to make derogatory remarks about anything they do themselves, even when these achievements are of a satisfactory standard. In addition, they are more likely to be ashamed of themselves, to have guilt feelings, to be depressed, to have a higher level of anxiety, to find everyday experiences unusually stressful, and to have a higher incidence of serious emotional difficulties.

Margaret Donaldson, a psychologist with a particular interest in the way children's minds develop, argues that a child can only establish a strong self-concept when she feels she is effective, competent and independent. A child with special needs may have weaknesses in precisely these areas, and so her self-esteem may be lower as a result. Her self-esteem may be further at risk because of the differences she perceives between herself and others.

Despite this, the evidence that children with special needs are more likely to experience emotional disturbance is ambiguous. One series of psychological studies concluded that apart from children with cerebral palsy (a condition caused by various forms of brain damage), emotional disturbance is only slightly more frequent among children with special needs than in the ordinary population. Other research investigations have found, for example, that children with spina bifida are likely to experience particular emotional and behavioural problems, such as passivity and lack of drive, distractibility in teaching situations, and anxiety when faced with problems.

COMPONENTS OF THE SELF-CONCEPT

Part of a child's self-concept is derived from the way other people react towards her. A child who constantly experiences a teaching situation in which she is regularly told that she is failing may give up trying at school. A girl who is constantly reminded that she is not well-coordinated may be afraid to embark on sporting activities. Insensitive reactions from other children and adults may negatively influence the self-perception of a child with special needs.

Yet the reactions of others can also work positively for children with special needs. Down's Syndrome causes very distinct facial features which makes the child immediately identifiable. Adults who associate the condition with limited development will instantly have lower expectations of such a child. However, as mentioned in Chapter 1, controversial medical research has used reconstructive facial surgery to make children with Down's Syndrome look less distinctive, more like the general population, in the hope that this might result in an all-round improvement is their development. Results have been encouraging – the children who have undergone this surgery function better and more independently in society. One explanation for this is that because a child with Down's syndrome, after cosmetic surgery, looks more 'normal', other children and adults interact more normally with her. The child's self-image is enhanced as a result of this new social reaction towards her, and consequently she is more able to cope with the demands of her environment.

Starting playgroup, nursery or school can be stormy for the child with special needs, since this may be the first time she interacts with people outside her immediate family. Throughout her early development, her parents will have spent a great deal of time encouraging her to cope by using the skills she has. A child who has limited movement in her legs will have been shown how to move around the house using arm-tripods, a wheelchair, or whatever. A child who has a cleft palate and unclear speech will have been shown how to make her voice as clear as possible. Within the home, the child will probably have a good self-image, and be full of self-confidence.

Stepping outside the confines of the family environment, the child is likely to come into contact with other children and adults who are not as supportive as her parents. She will meet people who stare at her, people who go out of their way to avoid her because they feel uncomfortable in her presence, and people who ask her questions about her difficulties. These reactions can have an adverse effect on the child, reducing her confidence and lowering her self-esteem. Try to discuss some possible reactions of others with your child, before she attends nursery or school. Of course, much depends on the level of your child's understanding. But where appropriate, you should explain that other children may not understand the effects of her disability, and that as a result they may say things that will upset her. At the same time, you should emphasize your child's strengths, for instance, that she has a pleasing personality, that she is cooperative, or that she is bright and inquisitive. A small amount of preparation before the child ventures into the outside world can help prevent her self-image from taking a tumble once she crosses the threshold of home.

Another influence on the development of a child's self-image is the extent to which she compares herself to other children of her own age. This type of self-comparison is a natural part of development, allowing a child to judge the strength of her own qualities and skills in relation to those of children she knows. That helps the child evaluate herself. Parents of a child with special needs are often faced with the dilemma of whether to have their child interact with other children who have special needs, on the basis that this will prevent her from inferior self-comparisons, or to have her interact with ordinary children, on the basis that this will encourage her to achieve more because of the higher standards being achieved by these children. In most instances, however, the latter sort of social interaction has a positive effect. Negative effects are likely only when the developmental gap between the child with special needs and the others is immense.

Girls with special needs tend to have a significantly lower level of self-esteem than boys with special needs. Psychologists explain this phenomenon on the basis that girls – in comparison to boys – place a greater emphasis on comparing themselves with friends and other children their own age. Girls also tend to place a higher value on physical attractiveness than boys do. However, this boy–girl difference in self-image does not usually emerge until the child is at least eight years old.

A child's self-image is also affected by her physical appearance. A child whose appearance conforms to the ideal view of the 'good-looking' child is more likely to have a positive self-concept than is a child whose appearance is untypical. But children with special needs and ordinary children share the same system of values about physical attractiveness and personal appearance. In other words, both groups of children have the same ideas about their ideal body shape. The self-image of a child with a physical disability, therefore, can be particularly low.

This distortion in self-image may be reflected in children's drawings of themselves. Ask a child who is physically disabled to draw a self-portrait. You may find that she actually draws a picture of herself in which the physical disability is either ignored altogether (the child draws herself without the disability), or concealed (the child draws herself behind a fence so that only her head shows), or even exaggerated (her leg calipers are presented disproportionately large).

Everybody has different roles in life, and this too affects the development of the self-image. You play out a wide range of roles, such as the role of parent, or partner, or colleague, or best friend, and so on. Each role makes different demands on you, requiring you to act in different ways, and affecting the way you see yourself. In each role you learn new information about yourself and your capabilities. Sometimes this information is positive (when, in the role of manager, you learn that you are capable of solving complex problems at work). Sometimes the information is negative (when, in the role of parent, you learn that you are unable to control your two-year-old's behaviour). All this information is integrated into your self-concept. A young child is no different from you in this respect. It is true that her roles (as child, friend and pupil) are less complex than most adult roles, but they have equal impact on the way she sees herself.

Many childhood roles, however, require normal development. The role of 'learner in the classroom' requires a child to be able to grasp certain fundamental cognitive concepts. The role of 'playground friend' might require a child to be able to move round the playground at the same rate as her classmates. The role of 'the child who relates her school experiences to her parents' requires that a child has to be able to use speech competently. Many of the normal roles of childhood, therefore, are not easily accessible to a child with special needs.

In addition, a child with special needs may be forced to fulfil roles not normally associated with childhood. She may gradually adopt the role of 'someone needing extra help with reading', the role of 'someone visiting the doctor frequently', or the role of 'the child who sits out of PE classes'. Having to fulfil untypical childhood roles can result in a self-image which varies from that normally found in children of the same age.

The last major component of a child's self-concept derives from the process of identification. Every child identifies with people in her life, usually her mother and father, but she can also identify with her friends and other adults that she knows. Through this, a child begins to adopt the ideas and behaviour of the person with whom she is identifying, and this in turn influences the feelings of personal worth the child has for herself. Therefore, parental attitudes – about the child's difficulties, about the way she should be managed at home, and so on – directly affect the way she sees herself.

PARENTS

Although these factors all play a part in the formation of a child's self-image, parents exert the most significant influence. The link between a mother's concept of her child and the child's own self-concept is particularly strong. Children who have a strong self-image tend to have parents who have a strong self-image themselves, who are psychologically stable and settled, who are able to cope with life, who appear calm under pressure, and who have clear ideas on the way children should be brought up.

Parent–child interactions have also been found to be crucial. Mothers of children with a strong self-concept are usually more accepting of the child's strengths and weaknesses. The mother and her child are able to communicate well and can convey loving emotions easily to each other. This type of mother is interested in her child's day-to-day experiences, and makes an effort to help her child achieve any task she is attempting. Parents who are derogatory about their child, or even indifferent about their relationships with her, will not encourage her to feel positively about herself. Coming to terms with the individuality of a child with special needs will enhance her own self-image.

Self-concept is also affected by the way parents maintain rules within the family home. Children with high self-esteem tend to have parents who are likely to enforce rules in the home consistently, and who prefer to use rewards to encourage the desired behaviour rather than punishments to discourage rule-breaking. These parents, even when they punish their child, do so in a manner that is straightforward and appropriate in intensity to the actual misdemeanour – they do not over-react. And they tend to respond quickly to their child's misbehaviour, rather than letting it go on for a long time until they can tolerate it no longer.

IMPROVING YOUR CHILD'S SELF-CONCEPT

You can help improve the self-concept of your child with special needs. The following suggestions will give you some direction:

- *Take an interest in all that your child does, in the minor as well as the major aspects of her day-to-day life.* Let your child see that you care about everything she does, whether it is how well she holds her cup for drinking, or how hard she is trying to master early reading skills.

- *Encourage your child to relate her daily experiences to you.* A child's natural desire to communicate with others exists whether her language development is adequate or not. You may not understand all that she says to you, but your interest in what she is trying to express to you will have a positive effect on her self-image.

- *Emphasize your child's strong points, especially when she feels she is not as capable as other children.* Whenever she compares herself to her friends, always encourage her to make these comparisons as broad as possible so that she does not focus on only one aspect. Point out to her that she has other characteristics that make her likeable, such as a pleasant manner and a caring attitude to others.

- *Always try to find some positive aspects of her behaviour and achievements that you can praise.* Even when your child misbehaves, don't repeatedly tell her how bad she is – constant reminders of her negative aspects will reduce her self-respect.

- *Make an effort to involve her in choices about minor matters in her life.* Encourage her to make decisions about small issues, such as what biscuits she eats, what juice she drinks, and so on. She may find that is a taxing responsibility but it will heighten her self-esteem eventually.

- *Provide experiences in which your child is likely to be successful, and avoid experiences in which you know she is bound to fail.* The best boost to a child's self-image is success. Your task is to find a level of activities which falls between asking too much of her (thereby presenting her repeatedly with failure) and too little of her (thereby lowering your expectations of her). The better you know your child as an individual, then the easier this becomes for you.

- *Develop clear ideas on the way your child should be managed at home.* Special needs or not, your child has the need to be brought up in a loving environment which has a clear and consistent structure. A home with rules that fluctuate from day to day is unlikely to promote a strong self-image.

- *Do not have one set of behavioural standards for your child with special needs and a totally different set for your other children.* Your child with special needs requires discipline as much as any of the others in your family (this is discussed in more detail in Chapter 10). Altering your usual standards of acceptance for child behaviour in the light of your child's particular developmental difficulties may result in her confusion. Having a completely different standard of behaviour for your child with special needs than you do for your other children may help create a self-image that emphasizes how different she is from others.

- *Talk to her about other children's reactions towards her.* You may be tempted to discourage discussion when your child mentions that her classmates have made fun of her because of the way she talks, or because she has learning difficulties – and this may partly be due to your own feelings of confusion about your child's problems. Far better to let her say what she feels, and to reassure her that these comments will become less frequent the more she ignores them.

THE SELF-FULFILLING PROPHECY

The self-fulfilling prophecy – the idea that if a person has specific expectations of us then we will behave in ways to confirm that expectation – can influence a child's self-image, which in turn can affect her progress. (This is discussed in more detail earlier, in Chapter 1.)

While it would be facile to suggest that your child with special needs could overcome all her developmental problems simply by your having high expectations of her, research does suggest that higher expectations of your child are more likely to lead to her success. That success need not only refer to educational achievements, but to all aspects of the child's development. A child with spina bifida who is allowed to use physical supports all the time may not feel the need to attempt to move in a more independent fashion. And a child with Down's Syndrome who is allowed to misbehave constantly because her parents assume that is part-and-parcel of her condition will not be motivated towards achieving a greater level of maturity.

7 · Speech and Language Difficulties

Many parents only become concerned about their child's development when they realize that his range and use of language are different from those of other children of his age. This realization may not occur until the parents have an opportunity to compare the child with others, perhaps at mother-and-toddler group, or at playgroup. Or it may arise from a relative's comments ('He seems slow to talk' or 'My friend's child is the same age and he talks much better than that'). Whatever the circumstances, a child's slow language development is often the first sign that he may have special needs. If you are anxious about possible language difficulties then you should seek professional advice through your health visitor or GP, who will refer your child to a psychologist or a speech therapist, depending on the nature of the child's difficulty.

RECEPTIVE AND EXPRESSIVE LANGUAGE

Language has an expressive component (the words the child uses, and the meaning he is trying to convey with these words) and a receptive component (the meaning that he extracts from language spoken to him). In all children, receptive language is well in advance of expressive language; for instance, a child who is unable to say his name may still may react with a smile when he hears his name being mentioned. That disparity by itself is not a cause for concern.

Receptive language develops at a faster rate because a child is bombarded with words long before he has the physical or intellectual capacity to speak. Right from birth he is stimulated by language, some of which is directed at him and some of which is an incidental part of his environment. And he is encouraged to respond to language before he is encouraged to speak. A mother who holds a bottle of milk up to her three-month-old baby and asks, 'Are you hungry? Would you like your bottle?' expects him to react positively by perhaps smiling, or waving his hands, or kicking his legs – she doesn't expect him to say, 'Yes, that would be lovely.'

Language development depends on a child's ability to make sense of what is happening around him. He has to be able to identify a specific object or event and then forge the connection between that and the word spoken at the same time. There is no logical reason, for example, why a bottle is called 'bottle' – it could just as easily be called 'house'. In order for a child to learn that the long, upright object with a liquid in it is called 'bottle', he has to be able to differentiate it from every other object in his surroundings; he has to be able to abstract the general concept of 'bottle-like objects' from all differently shaped bottles that he sees, and then he has to associate the specific word 'bottle' (which he himself can't use yet) with that concept. A child with special needs takes longer to form these connections between words and events because of his difficulties in comprehending the events in his everyday life. And hence there may be language difficulties.

NON-VERBAL COMMUNICATION

Although spoken language may eventually be your child's main means of communication, he will able to communicate his feelings non-verbally before he learns to talk.

A child's crying conveys many different moods. Many parents are able to tell when their infant's cry means he is in pain, when it means he is bored, and when it means he is hungry. Some parents even claim that they can tell when their child is unwell, just by the crying sounds he makes – when psychologists investigated this, they found that sick children have a higher-pitched cry than healthy children, supporting the parental observations.

Facial expressions and body gestures also play a part in non-verbal communication. A smile indicates pleasure. A child who has had enough to eat gets this message across to his parents easily by spitting out his food, or by pushing the plate away. And a child who does not like what he is asked to do may turn round and walk away without saying a word.

A child with special needs may continue to use non-verbal behaviour as his main means of communication for longer than usual. His delay in acquiring language means he has a strong dependence on using other ways to express his desires. Parents may have to pay more attention than they would normally to his cries, to his body movements, to his expressions and to his eye movements, since these are the channels through which their infant tries to make contact with them.

As a child matures, he will probably begin to move away from non-verbal communication towards using language. He may try to make sounds that have some similarity to word syllables, even though he cannot speak in actual words yet. Psychologists claim this causes a sense of frustration, which underlies many of the tantrums displayed by children with language difficulties. Parents often find their previously frustrated child becomes more settled once he can communicate using language rather than gestures.

HOW CHILDREN LEARN LANGUAGE

If you have ever tried to learn a second language yourself, as an adult, you will realize what a complex task this is. Imagine if the language you had to learn was English. There are thousands of words to be remembered, endless grammatical rules, and a long list of words with more than one meaning. Then there are words that sound the same but have different spelling patterns (their/there), and words that have similar spelling patterns but sound different (cough/bough). You would probably think it was an impossible task to master. It is almost as if we have been pre-programmed to learn language in a certain way, as if we are born with an innate ability to develop a meaningful language system.

This idea of an innate language ability is one theory psychologists use to explain how children learn language. This theory proposes that a baby is genetically endowed with a 'Language Acquisition Device' – an inborn device that predisposes the developing child to recognize certain types of words and grammatical structures when he hears them. The language acquisition device enables the child to pick out the important parts of the speech that he hears. The problem with this theory is that it suggests that the child's environment is unimportant since he will learn language in whatever context he is raised. But a child's language is greatly influenced by his family upbringing.

An alternative theory of language development comes from behaviourist psychologists who maintain that a child has no inborn notion of language whatsoever. Instead, the behaviourist argues that a child learns certain words and word structures because his parents reward him when he uses them. When the child points to a glass of juice and says the word 'juice', his parents smile, lavish praise on him for having used the word in its proper context, and then reward him even further by giving him the juice. That type of interaction, says the behaviourist, occurs many times every day and that is how a child learns to speak. The difficulty with this theory, however, is that it cannot explain why a child only picks out certain words from the hundreds of thousands he hears each day. And then there is the difficulty in explaining how a child can invent new words – for instance, the two-year-old who says 'milk gone-ded' – even though he has never been taught this by his parents in the past.

There seems to be an element of truth in both these theories, though neither is sufficient on its own. Language learning is probably a combination of inborn language skills and the effect of the child's environment. In many instances of language difficulty, no single cause can be identified.

MINOR SPEECH AND LANGUAGE DIFFICULTIES

A child may have a speech difficulty, even though all other areas of his development are satisfactory. In such cases the speech difficulty is the child's sole problem and either clears up spontaneously or else responds to help from a speech therapist.

Lisping is one of these minor difficulties. Children often develop a lisp in the pre-school years. They begin to make letter substitutes, such as 'th' for 's', 'f' for 'th', and so on. Fortunately, these speech patterns pass as the child matures, usually by the time he reaches school. A child might acquire a temporary lisp when his first teeth begin to fall out, but again this lasts only for a short while until his second teeth grow in. A lisp can also be caused by misuse of the tongue, or by a cleft palate. Speech therapy is helpful in these instances.

Mispronunciations are common in young children. Learning to speak takes time, and making mistakes is part of the learning process. Many children experience difficulty with certain sounds. This results in the child's speech being unclear. Again, this defect usually disappears spontaneously as the child becomes more mature and more experienced linguistically. If a child's speech is still unclear by the time he is nearing school age, then speech therapy may be required.

Lack of stimulation can sometimes result in a minor, and temporary, speech problem. Speech development depends partly on a child's interaction with others in his family. By listening to everyone in his family talking to him, the infant's interest in language is stimulated. He needs that type of individual attention to spur on his language acquisition. However, in certain circumstances this may not be readily available. The youngest child in a large family, a child who has a brother or sister close in age, or a child who is cared for by someone who speaks very little themselves, may suffer from lack of stimulation. Once this is identified as being the cause, the remedy is straightforward – lots of individual attention using discussions, stories, song and poems.

Stammering (also called stuttering) is another speech difficulty which concerns parents, but it is important not to over-react to this. With this defect, a child talks very hesitantly, perhaps repeating the first letter or first part of a word several times. It is almost as though the child is trying to sort out his thoughts while he stutters. Many children in the early stages of language acquisition develop some form of stutter, probably because there is so much they want to say all at once. This temporary form of speech impediment clears up as the child becomes more confident in his use of language. The cardinal rules when interacting with a stuttering child are: never make fun of him, never imitate him, and never become impatient with him – otherwise his stutter will simply become more extreme. Speech therapy techniques are able to help stutterers gain more control over their speech.

MAJOR LANGUAGE DIFFICULTIES

A child's speech and language difficulty, however, can be more serious. Surveys suggest that 5–15 per cent of children come into this category. The most frequent cause of serious language difficulties is a hearing loss, since adequate hearing is crucial for a child to learn language. If he cannot hear the sounds of speech, then he will not be able to reproduce them in his own speech. (This is discussed in more detail in Chapter 8.)

Slowness to develop language can be a sign of a general developmental delay. In these circumstances, the child will also be slow in learning to sit up on his own, in learning to walk, in learning bladder control, in becoming independent, and in learning to socialize with other children. The earlier this type of difficulty is detected then the sooner the child will be able to receive help to stimulate his development. Language delay can emerge in the child's receptive language: he may take longer than usual to discriminate between colours, he may fail to interpret non-verbal gestures, or he may have difficulties understanding the meaning of prepositional words such as 'in' and 'above'. It can also emerge in expressive language: the child may have a limited vocabulary, he may talk in single words when other children his own age are talking in sentences, or he may use words in the wrong context.

A very complex cause of language difficulties is a condition known as autism. An autistic child uses language in a bizarre way, so that normal communication with him is not possible. Michael Rutter, a leading British child psychiatrist, has defined the distinguishing characteristics of autism as delayed language development with impaired comprehension, a failure to form social relationships, and compulsive ritualistic behaviour. Autistic children may use very little language and appear emotionally distant from others around them. Although there is much disagreement among professionals over the true nature and cause of autism – many psychologists have long ceased to use the term, preferring to consider the syndrome as a communication disorder – Rutter argues that autism is caused by brain damage which impairs the child's ability to make sense out of the sounds he hears.

Some speech difficulties are definitely caused by brain damage. Specific areas of the brain are responsible for specific functions, and if the area responsible for language is damaged, then the child will have a language difficulty. The seriousness and extent of the problems depend on the degree of brain damage which has occurred. Cerebral palsy, a condition affecting approximately one child in 400, is an umbrella term used to describe a wide range of conditions which have two things in common; they are all caused by damage to part of the child's brain, and they all result in the child having difficulties with balance, posture, coordination and movement. Many children with cerebral palsy also have speech and language problems. The brain damage causing cerebral palsy can occur when the foetus is in the womb (when the mother becomes infected in early pregnancy by German measles, cytomegalovirus or toxiplasmosis), during the birth process (when a baby is deprived of oxygen for a short time during labour), or even after the birth (as a result of severe jaundice, or meningitis).

In some instances a severe articulation disorder can seriously impair language development; a child may have problems in actually producing speech sounds, even though he may know what he wants to say and how it should sound. Mild articulation errors are a normal part of development. Many two-year-olds miss out parts of words (saying 'at' for 'cat', or 'do' for 'dog') or may substitute one sound for another (saying 'toat' for 'coat' or 'foon' for 'spoon'). However, severe articulation disorders lasting well beyond the preschool years may render the older child's language totally unintelligible.

HELPING YOUR CHILD'S LANGUAGE

Early intervention, involving proper identification, assessment and treatment procedures, is vital. Be extremely cautious about accepting the 'he'll grow out of it' statement. A high number of parents who draw attention to their young child's speech and language difficulty are told to wait a few months, or even years, in the hope that the problem will be self-correcting. That can happen, but in most instances a child will benefit from some form of language programme, ranging from intensive regular speech therapy to language games at home. If in doubt, insist your GP refers your child for specialist assessment.

The following strategies will help you encourage your child during the early stages of language development, when he is unable to use single words:

- *Make use of early non-verbal communication.* This is the precursor of language as a channel of communication. Position your face so that your child can see the different expressions you make. Hanging stimulating mobiles over his cot or bed also encourages him to look closely at his surroundings.

- *Talk to your child.* You may feel foolish talking to a child who appears to have no idea what you are saying, but even at that very early stage, parental speech is an important stimulus. It allows him to see that language has a purpose, it stimulates his interest and develops his listening skills. You will find as he matures that he begins to imitate your sounds.

- *Make lots of different sounds.* That will encourage him to develop listening skills. A bell ringing, keys jingling, his rattle being shaken, voices ranging from a whisper to a raised tone, are only a few of the many sounds that will attract his attention. The better he is at listening to noises in his environment, the sooner he will start to experiment with these sounds himself.

- *Respond to any sounds he makes.* A child uses a wide variety of sounds when babbling. Sometimes these sounds are just for his own pleasure, especially when he is playing alone, but most times they are used to attract your attention. The more you respond to his vocalizations then the more likely he is to continue making them.

- *Read story books to him.* Even a child who has no formal speech of his own will enjoy having stories read to him. This stimulates his interest in language, and also in books. The closeness of parent and child during storytime is another incentive to language development.

In the next stage of language development, when the child is beginning to use identifiable words, the following techniques are also useful:

- *Encourage your child to listen to songs, music and poems.* These will provide him with another source of amusement and at the same time he is likely to attempt to sing along. Filling in the last word of a nursery rhyme is also a popular game for the young child who is beginning to speak. Language games, such as 'round and round the garden', are also very popular with young children, as are action rhymes such as 'I'm a little teapot'.

- *Talk to him in your usual voice.* There is no need to modify your words to include baby-talk. The child has as much chance of understanding what 'dog' means as he has of understanding what 'bow-wow' means. All that baby-talk teaches a child is a language which he will have to modify as soon as he matures. Talk to your child using your normal voice. He will gradually pick out the important words from your speech.

- *Let him look at himself in a mirror when he is making sounds.* That will allow him to see that his mouth actually moves in specific ways when he makes particular sounds. Your child may derive great pleasure from watching the strange shapes his mouth makes, and this may motivate him to make an even broader range of sounds.

- *Give your child a chance to speak.* It is all too easy in families to relegate the children's language to second place. At the end of a difficult day, you have lots of information to exchange with your partner. But your child also needs to be given an opportunity to speak. Let him tell you his news, however trivial that may be when compared to your own experiences that day, and however long it may take for him to make himself understood. Ask him questions about what he tells you. Even the child who has only a few words of speech will thrive under that form of parental attention.

- *Avoid constantly correcting your child when he makes a mistake in his speech.* Learning language takes time and it is only natural that a child should have some difficulties along the way. Continual correction of errors will reduce your child's confidence, and make him reluctant to talk at all.

- *Take the advice of your child's speech therapist.* Speech therapists are specially trained to assess children with speech difficulties, and use specialized tests to pinpoint the areas of difficulties. Most children enjoy this type of assessment because it involves playing with toys. Having identified why your child's speech is not as advanced as it should be, the speech therapist will then arrange to see him regularly in order to provide him with a range of language activities. However, she will also give you lots of tasks to do with your child at home, some of them mouth, tongue and lip exercises, others more general. All of these should be carried out. And make sure there is always an element of fun when you are helping your child – your impatience will only make him tense and anxious.

8 · Hearing Difficulties

Hearing loss, whether total or partial, is the single most common cause of a child's failure to develop normal speech. Approximately one child in ten has a mild hearing loss, and approximately one child per 1,000 has a severe hearing loss or total deafness. Some conditions affecting development have associated hearing difficulties; for instance, in 1974, a study of over 100 children with Down's Syndrome discovered a high incidence of hearing loss. Almost 90 per cent of deaf children have parents with normal hearing, and consequently are raised in an environment in which speech is the main mode of communication.

A baby with hearing impairment has a number of difficulties. First, she cannot hear the everyday sounds which stimulate a baby with normal hearing. Second, she gets no feedback from her own speech because she cannot hear the sounds she is making. A deaf baby starts to make sounds at around the same age as a hearing baby, but the lack of feedback means she has less encouragement to practise and enlarge her range of vocalizations. And third, she cannot hear what is being said to her by other children and adults. Hearing difficulties impair the child's ability to interact with other people, and can cause a sense of isolation.

Babbling and listening to sounds provide the foundation for later speech development. A child who misses out on these early experiences as a baby will find that learning to speak is harder than it is for a child with normal hearing. A child with hearing impairment may be slower to speak, she may not use her first words until long after the age she is expected to, and she may be slower to understand the meaning of words. The sooner a hearing loss is identified, then the sooner action can be taken to help the child – the longer a child's hearing loss goes undetected, then the greater will be the delay in her language learning.

CAUSES OF HEARING LOSS

In a normal human hearing system, sound gets picked up by the outer ear, then passes on to the eardrum through the ear canal. This activates the small bones in the middle ear, passing the sound on to the cochlea where it changes into electrical impulses. These electrical impulses are rather like messages which pass along the nerve of hearing to the brain. Problems can arise in any part of this system, resulting in some hearing loss.

Researchers have presented sounds of different volume, frequency and duration to newborn babies, and have examined their reactions (as judged by the changes in the baby's heart-rate, facial expressions and respiration). The outcome of these studies suggests that a newborn baby with normal hearing can detect differences in noise tone and sound frequency. Newborn babies generally prefer short bursts of noise to long continuous sounds, and they find rhythmic sounds more relaxing. All these auditory skills are part of the foundations of later language development in the child with normal hearing.

The cause of hearing defects, and even of profound deafness, cannot always be traced – something clearly dissatisfying for parents who naturally want an explanation of their child's hearing difficulty. Hearing difficulties can originate during pregnancy (for instance, where the foetus has been impaired by infection, such as German measles), or during the birth (perhaps due to lack of oxygen at critical moments), or after birth (as a result of head injury or illness). Certain conditions of deafness can also be inherited.

There are two categories of hearing loss. First, there is *conductive deafness*, which is treatable. In this condition, sound is prevented from reaching the inner ear from the outer and middle ear. A blockage of wax in the ear canal can result in temporary deafness; an American survey found that almost 15 per cent of all children had both ears blocked in this way. 'Swimmer's ear', resulting from bacteria and water trapped by earwax, is another cause of conductive hearing loss, as is middle-ear infection which often arises from the common cold. Medical treatment from the family doctor usually resolves conductive hearing loss.

Second, there is *perceptive deafness*, which is much more serious because it usually cannot be cured. This condition arises from extreme damage to either the inner ear, or the hearing nerve, or that part of the brain responsible for hearing. Perceptive hearing loss is often congenital. The majority of children with this type of hearing impairment have some residual hearing and therefore are likely to benefit from using a hearing-aid. If your child does have a hearing difficulty, then your doctor will probably explain all this to you. But don't be afraid to ask.

SIGNS OF HEARING LOSS

Hearing loss is difficult for parents to detect because the baby cannot indicate her difficulty. As far as the baby with partial hearing is concerned, hearing muffled sounds is normal. Therefore parents have to look for behavioural signs that something is wrong. If you are concerned that your baby may not be hearing properly, ask yourself the following questions:

- *Does she respond to your voice?* Your baby should show an almost immediate reaction when you speak to her, either by turning her head towards you or else by at least showing some change in her behaviour at the time. Failure, or slowness, to react could be important.
- *Does your baby seem to be soothed by your voice if you are not in her line of vision?* Most babies when distressed will be soothed by their mother's comforting voice and will become calmer. However, the baby with hearing impairment may only be soothed when she can actually see her mother.
- *Is your baby startled when someone comes into her line of vision?* Babies with normal hearing soon learn to anticipate the arrival of another person by the sounds they make. Footsteps coming closer, or the noise of the bedroom door opening, are sounds a

hearing baby uses to judge that someone is coming up to her. A child with a hearing disability has no such anticipatory cues and hence may be alarmed when somebody suddenly appears in her line of vision.

- *Do your baby's sounds continue to progress after the age of six months?* Even up to the age of six months, a baby with hearing impairment will make the normal range of sounds despite the fact she cannot hear them herself. However, whereas a hearing baby's sounds continue to increase and become more elaborate after that age, a deaf baby's speech does not, and she may even use her voice less.

- *Can your baby locate a sound source?* By the age of two months, a baby with normal hearing will react to a sound by turning her eyes or head towards it. Try talking to your baby or shaking a rattle when she is not looking at you – but do it gently or you may frighten her. The partially-hearing or deaf baby will not respond or else may seem confused because she cannot tell where the sound is coming from.

- *Does your baby always turn the same ear towards a sound-source, irrespective of the direction of the noise?* If so, she may have a hearing loss in one ear only. A baby with normal hearing will turn the left or right side of her head towards a sound, depending on the direction it is coming from.

As a baby becomes older, detection of hearing loss becomes easier. The hearing child age three years and upwards will interact happily with her friends and family, whereas the partially-hearing or deaf child will not have such a well-developed system of communication. Some of the following indicators of hearing loss could also be due to the child's egocentricity or disobedience, but you should still look out for them:

- *Does your child respond quickly and accurately to a simple request?* A young child should be able to react quickly to a basic command. Of course, your child may be pretending not to hear you but if this happens consistently there may be a hearing difficulty.

- *Does your child stop when she is told to and come to you when asked?* If not, this behaviour may again be a sign of your child's unwillingness to cooperate with you. But repeated instances of this behaviour may be a sign of a partial hearing loss.

- *Do you find that you have to repeat questions all the time to your child before she responds?* The child with normal hearing should be able to interpret questions that are put to her, without them having to be repeated. The child with partial hearing can be very confused in question-and-answer situations.
- *Does your child watch your face and mouth very closely during a conversation with her?* A child with hearing loss needs other cues to understand what you are saying, apart from the actual words you are using. She may rely on lip reading and other facial signs to make sense of what she is hearing.
- *Is your child's speech development delayed?* Not every speech defect is caused by hearing difficulties, although many are. There are several vocal characteristics more common in the speech of children with partial hearing than in the speech of children with normal hearing; for example, speech will be of low quality with the ends of words missing, the range of the child's vocabulary will be restricted in comparison to other children her age, she may mix up letters in her speech (such as 't' and 'k', or 'd' and 'g') and there may be no detectable difference in her words between the 'sh' and 's' sounds.
- *Does she have a high level of frustration?* The child with partial, or total, hearing loss usually becomes easily frustrated because she cannot understand what is going on. Tantrums in a young child are part of normal development, but severe tantrums, in conjunction with some of the other signs, may reflect a hearing difficulty.

None of the above indicators by themselves necessarily mean that the child has a hearing loss, since lack of responsiveness could be due to the child's temperament. However, should you find the above mentioned patterns of behaviour are being repeated every day, then discuss the matter with your GP. A survey on hearing loss showed that in three cases out of four, the difficulty was first suspected by the child's parents whereas only one case in twenty was first suspected by a doctor. And be prepared to persevere. One survey looked at referrals of possible hearing loss to family doctors, and found that half of all family doctors consulted by parents of children who were later found to be deaf, did not agree the child was deaf. A third of these doctors refused referral to a specialist. Once a child reaches a specialist, far fewer omissions are made.

HEARING TESTS AND SPECIALIST ASSESSMENT

Routine hearing checks are given soon after birth. These checks are repeated again when the baby is around six months old, at the local child health clinic, and again at regular intervals throughout the pre-school years. Tests are carried out by a health visitor or doctor. When this very basic screening suggests that a child has some hearing loss, she will be referred for more detailed assessment at an audiology clinic, which has specialized equipment available. This involves the child being presented with sounds at varying – but finely controlled – frequencies, and each of the child's responses is noted. An audiogram (graph) showing the profile of the child's hearing is then drawn in order to show at which frequencies the hearing loss, if any, is occurring. Children referred for speech therapy are always given a full audiological assessment.

Once a hearing difficulty is diagnosed, you will find that the assessment is continuous, and is repeated regularly throughout childhood, because hearing levels can fluctuate. To determine what help is required to meet the special needs of a child with partial hearing, the professionals involved need to establish the full extent of her residual hearing, what hearing-aids would be most suitable for her, what her level of language development is, and the level of her comprehension. These pieces of information enable the hearing loss to be seen within the wider context of the child's general development – but this means you will see many different people. Don't be discouraged by this.

Each one of these professionals has a particular contribution to make towards helping your child manage her hearing difficulty. An otologist is an ENT (ear, nose and throat) medical consultant, specializing in diseases affecting the ear, who will be in charge of medical treatment for your child's condition; an audiometrician is a specialist who conducts the audiometric assessment, and who may be involved in fitting hearing-aids; a teacher of the deaf is a specially trained teacher who works with children with impaired hearing and their families, advising on the child's educational needs; and an educational psychologist is a psychologist trained in child development, as well as being a qualified teacher, who will assess the child's progress regularly, advising accordingly.

ENCOURAGING LANGUAGE DEVELOPMENT IN A CHILD WITH HEARING IMPAIRMENT

Parents have a major role to play in determining the full effect of their child's hearing difficulty. A child with hearing loss has the right to participate in her family along with her brothers and sisters. She should be allowed the same opportunities for self-development and be allowed to establish her independence and self-confidence. The way you respond to your child at home will greatly influence her ability to cope. All those suggestions for stimulating language development given in the previous chapter, also apply to the child with a hearing loss. In addition, the following points will provide you with further ideas:

- *Use toys to help stimulate your child's interest.* In the early weeks of life, a baby will be aware of a rattle hanging near her. If hearing loss has been diagnosed at this age, choose a rattle that is brightly coloured, and one that lets her feel vibrations when it is shaken. At around six months, when the child is able to sit on her own, music often has great appeal. A solid toy music box or portable radio held close to the child will enable her to actually feel beat and rhythm. Towards the end of the first year, games that present different sounds in different places will be useful, for instance, peek-a-boo with all sorts of musical instruments encourages the child to locate noises. Past this age, toy shops are full of games that provide learning, language and listening experiences.
- *Make sure your child wears a hearing-aid if it has been prescribed by the ENT consultant.* Hearing-aids can make sounds louder for the listener, though a deaf child will still not hear words exactly as a child with normal hearing does. Your child may not be comfortable wearing the aid and she may feel embarrassed by it, but the

aid should be worn continually at the correct adjustment. Modern hearing-aids are extremely powerful, and can offer substantial help to a child with hearing loss.

- *Make meaningful conversation with your child.* Resist the temptation to be stilted and exaggerated when conversing with a child who has a hearing difficulty. Your child must see that speaking has a purpose – and a dull, unenthusiastic exchange of words is unlikely to give her that impression. Make a special effort to understand what she has to say. Continued failure to communicate increases the child's frustration and anger.

- *Don't make your child repeat everything she says.* Instead, say back to the child what she has been trying to communicate to you. For example, if she indicates that she wants a glass of juice, then you should say, 'You want a glass of juice?' That way she will be able hear the proper words and learn from them.

- *Use mature speech.* Some adults talk to a child who has partial hearing at the level of the child's language, not of the child's age or intellect. This means the child hears babyish speech from you. Better not to modify your own speech in this manner. Always speak using your normal language structures.

- *Be sensitive to your child's social and emotional development.* Deaf children are more prone to behaviour problems than are hearing children because communication is such a struggle for them. Frustrations build up easily. But that does not mean a child with hearing loss should be pitied. Treat your child who has a hearing difficulty as you treat your other children – that is the best way to encourage her all-round development.

9 · Visual Difficulties

Although total blindness in childhood is rare, many children have sufficiently bad eyesight to require some form of visual aid over and above the normal range of glasses obtainable on prescription from a High Street optician.

Sight is only one of five senses, yet it is possibly the most important, since a great deal of learning takes place through vision. A baby uses his eyes to explore the environment; an infant uses vision to judge the expression on his mother's face; a toddler uses sight as he wanders about the room, avoiding the hazards as he goes; a pre-schooler uses vision to fit the pieces into his shape-sorter; a school-age child uses sight to learn to read. In fact, vision is central to a child's development, and a child with impaired vision may be slower to learn basic skills than a sighted child.

Typical age-related visual skills are given in the Visual-Motor Development Section of the Developmental Checklists in Appendix I at the end of this book. Visual-motor skills are involved in coordinating eye and hand movements, including the extent to which a child can pick up and hold small objects, use hand implements, and control a pencil when drawing or writing.

VISUAL DEVELOPMENT

William James, one of the first ever psychologists, believed that a baby was born with very little visual ability. He described a new baby's visual experiences as a 'buzzing, booming confusion'. But we now know James was wrong.

Pioneer research into the vision of newborn babies was started in the 1950s by Robert Fantz, at the University of Chicago. He constructed the 'looking chamber', a large box-like apparatus in which the baby lies flat on his back looking up at various objects suspended from the box's ceiling. The investigator stands over the chamber looking directly down into the baby's eyes, enabling his eye movements to be monitored.

Results from these studies demonstrated that a young baby arrives into the world already pre-programmed to attend to specific features in the environment. At birth, a new baby is sensitive to light. If a very bright light shines into a baby's eyes, he will shut them tightly and keep them that way until the light source is removed. A newborn baby can also track large moving objects. He is able to notice movements of large shapes, and may watch his mother as she crosses from one side of the room to the other. He is able to detect contours; when a new baby is shown a solid black shape against a contrasting white background, he will spend most time looking at the points where black and white meet. A new baby prefers patterns to colours; he will look longer at a patterned picture than he will at a solid-colour picture. He naturally focuses on objects between 8 and 10 inches away from his face – this means a baby can look closely at his mother's face while she is feeding him. And he acquires basic depth perception (seeing three-dimensional objects) within a few hours of birth.

Some psychologists – in particular, Gordon Bronson – argue that a major change in the way an infant uses vision occurs at around the age of two months. Until then, a baby uses his 'secondary visual system' and is concerned only with the whereabouts of an object. So a baby younger than two months will watch an object as it moves around, will focus on something that comes near to him, and will look at the edges of things.

After that, a baby's 'primary visual system' takes over and he now becomes more interested in what an object actually is. The baby starts to attend more to details, such as whether the object is straight or curved, light or dark, and so on; and instead of peering at only one specific feature of a picture (as does the very young baby), an infant of two months or older begins to scan the whole picture.

These early visual skills enable a new baby to begin to make sense of the world around him, to distil meaning from all that is happening in his immediate environment. Lack of these visual skills hampers this process. There is also a social dimension to visual impairment. The baby will not be able to see the wide range of facial expressions used by his mother during feeding and changing, nor be able to respond to them. In this way the normal channels of non-verbal communication between a mother and her young baby are not readily available with a baby who only has partial sight, and this situation will continue throughout childhood.

THE EYE

In comparison to an adult, a baby's eyes are large in relation to the size of his head. In fact, a baby's eyes are almost 65 per cent the size of adult eyes. That is why some adults find babies so attractive – their disproportionately large eyes can seem very appealing.

The visible part of the eye is covered with a thin, delicate and transparent membrane – the conjunctiva – which extends to line the inside of the eyelid. Fluid produced by the tear gland washes the eyeball and keeps it well lubricated. Underneath the conjunctiva, at the front of the eye, lies the cornea, a disc-shaped part of the eye which bends the light as it enters. The cornea also protects the parts of the eye lying directly behind it. It is extremely sensitive, with in-built actions to remove any bits of dirt that land on it. The eye itself is filled with fluid, known as vitreous humour.

The iris – the coloured portion of the eye – lies behind the cornea. This has a dark hole in the middle, the pupil, which is controlled by lots of very small muscles, and light enters the eye through this. Just like the aperture of a camera, the pupil adjusts constantly in relation to the degree of light – in bright sunlight, the pupil becomes smaller, and in dim light it becomes larger.

Immediately behind the iris is the transparent and solid lens, whose muscles adjust its shape in order to focus light rays on to the light-sensitive retina at the back of the eye. When cells in the retina are activated, visual impulses are transmitted along the optic nerve to the brain. At that point, they are transformed into an image. Thus accurate vision is a complex process, involving many variables.

Damage to any part of the eye, or any part of the nervous system linking the eye to the brain, will result in visual impairment.

VISUAL DIFFICULTIES

A visual defect can manifest itself in a number of different ways. Vision may be blurred and distorted. With this condition, it is as if the child is looking at life through a pane of frosted glass. Close-up vision does not present a problem, but distant vision does. When playing, the child may be able to pick out the outlines of other children, but he cannot actually see who they are.

There may be a loss of central vision, in which the child cannot see an object directly in front of him. He may only be able to see out of the side of his eyes, so that he has to turn his head at an angle when trying to look at something. Running around is no problem, but reading is.

Tunnel vision results from a loss of peripheral vision, and the child may only be able to see a small part of what is in front of him, as if he is looking through a pin-hole in a piece of blank paper. Consequently, he may have difficulties moving around without bumping into things.

When there is a loss of visual field, a very specific part of the child's vision may be impaired. For instance, he may only be able to see from the centre out to the right-hand side in each eye, and be unable to see anything from the centre to the left-hand side.

There are many causes of visual impairment in childhood. The more severe ones include, first, cataracts. This is an opaqueness in all or part of the lens (the word 'cataract' comes from the Latin word meaning waterfall). For instance, a child may be born with cataracts (congenital cataracts) when the mother had German measles during pregnancy, or he may acquire cataracts later on through an injury to the eye. Corrective surgical work is possible, but this is rare for a baby unless the ophthalmic surgeon believes there is a genuine risk of blindness in both eyes.

Second, glaucoma (buphthalmos). A baby suffers from this when the fluid that occurs naturally in the eye cannot drain away. This build-up of liquid causes an unnatural pressure on the eye, resulting in blurred vision. Proper treatment can remedy the potential loss of sight.

A third cause of severe visual difficulty in children is a squint (strabismus). When this occurs, a child's eyes appear to look in opposite directions, and it means that he cannot stare at the same object with both eyes at the one time. In a young baby under the age of six months, a squint is normal. However, if a squint continues and is untreated until the child is two or three years of age, then blindness in one eye may occur. Treatment for squints varies from covering up the good eye (to force the muscles of the squinting eye to work properly) to surgery (to alter the length of the eye muscles).

Fourth, toxocariasis – a rare disease passed to children through contact with dog or cat excrement, usually when the infant is paying in a public park or garden used by animals – can result in blindness. If a toddler touches worm eggs that have been passed from infected cats or dogs, and then puts his hands into his mouth, the eggs may subsequently find their way into his intestines. That is one reason why dogs and cats should be kept away from children's play areas.

Finally, nystagmus is a condition in which the eyes have an involuntary flicking movement, frequently from side to side, but sometimes up and down. Nystagmus usually interferes with distance vision, while near vision may be unaffected.

There are many children with much less serious visual defects. But there is little cause for concern because the wearing of prescription glasses remedies the child's difficulty. Common remediable defects include short-sightedness (the child sees objects that are near but an object far away, for example, the blackboard, will appear blurred) and long-sightedness (the child sees objects far away clearly whereas a nearby object, for example, a writing jotter, will appear blurred). Although short-sightedness is more common than long-sightedness, both conditions can affect school performance. Astigmatism – where the eye is misshapen, producing a distorted image on the retina – can impair reading.

VISUAL ASSESSMENT

As with hearing, the vision of most children is tested regularly as a matter of routine in the pre-school years, and again when the child starts primary schooling. This form of assessment ensures that visual defects are identified – and corrected – as soon as possible, with minimum interference to the child's development. Vision testing can be done with children of all ages, but it takes time. The child needs to be relaxed and responsive. If your child is uncooperative during an eyesight test, make sure you arrange another appointment. Some parents regard these tests as a waste of time because they think they would be able to spot visual defects in their own child quite easily. But that is not always the case. Routine screening is a worthwhile and efficient means of detecting these minor visual defects.

BONDING

Psychological research into bonding between mothers and their babies has shown that severe visual defects can actually have an adverse effect on the formation of early emotional attachments. Comparing babies who are blind or who have partial sight with babies of normal sight, the following important differences were found:

- Whereas both sets of babies give their first smile at around the same age, babies with partial sight smile less frequently and less intensely.
- Whereas a baby with normal vision makes regular eye-contact with his mother and father during feeding or playing, the baby with partial sight does not enter into this habit of mutual gazing.
- Whereas a baby with full sight usually has a wide range of facial expressions to indicate his mood, the baby with partial sight has a narrower range and appears more sombre and morose. Parents of blind children often comment that before the difficulty was identified, they thought their baby was suffering from depression.

These differences in patterns of communication mean that the baby with partial sight and his mother are at a disadvantage when trying to form an emotional connection. One study looked at the interactions between mothers and their babies with partial sight. The researchers found that although the mothers were able to meet their baby's physical needs, by washing, feeding and changing him, they tended not to play with their baby nor did they try to encourage him to smile at them. However, the researchers were able to teach these mothers how to communicate with their baby in other ways, for instance, by attending to the infant's hand and body movements. These measures were successful in enhancing the mother–child relationship.

MANAGING A CHILD WITH VISUAL DIFFICULTIES

A baby has to learn to use whatever vision he has, no matter how slight that may be. Unlike the baby with normal vision who can sit unaided and use his eyes to observe his environment, a baby with visual difficulties needs the environment to come to him. Objects have to be brought close to him, people have to be nearer than normal when talking to him. A baby with partial sight needs a lot more touching and physical communication with his parents, and will rely on various sounds and smells to gain understanding of what is going on around him.

Just like a normal baby, a baby with visual difficulties needs to be placed in different positions in order to encourage his physical development. He should have the opportunity to be in his pram, in his walker, in his buggy and in his 'relaxer'. He should also be allowed to experience rolling about on the floor. And, of course, adults and children should talk to him while playing with him.

Parents of a child with visual difficulties often become very protective when he reaches the toddler stage. Understandably, they are concerned that their youngster will hurt himself. But he should be allowed to roam freely around his environment. As long as sensible safely precautions are taken (such as using a cooker guard, putting a rail across the top of the stairs, using covers for the electric sockets, etc.) then the few bumps and bruises that he acquires will be more than offset by the benefit he gains from exploring his surroundings.

Language is crucial for the pre-school child with a visual defect. He needs to be spoken to as often as possible, to be told what is going on, why he is being taken from here to there, what the other people in the room are doing, where the smells are coming from, and so on. This encourages the child to take an interest in what is happening, and also stimulates his desire to ask questions himself. This will only increase his self-confidence.

Toys are as important to the development of a child who has partial sight as they are to a child who has normal vision, although buying a toy for a child with limited vision requires a bit more thought. There are specialist toys designed specifically for children with visual difficulties but these are not readily sold in most toy shops, and so toys will have to be selected from the range normally available. Some special toys are available through toy libraries (see National Toy Libraries Association in Appendix III). When selecting a toy for a child with partial sight, the following points should be considered:

- *Stimulating*. The child will prefer toys that are interesting to touch, that rattle or make any sort of noise when played with, and that even have an interesting smell.
- *Colourful*. Even a child with severe visual difficulties may have some vision, however slight. Brightly coloured toys, in vivid yellow, blue, red or green, are easier to see.
- *Play potential*. Some toys, such as jigsaws, are only usable in specific ways, whereas other toys, such as building bricks, can be used by the child in a variety of ways. This latter group of toys, with a greater play potential, are most suited to the needs of a child with partial sight.
- *Purposeful*. Toys aimed at developing specific skills, for instance, form-boards, finger-puppets, pedal cars and shape-sorters, are as appropriate for the partially-sighted child as they are for the ordinary child.
- *Safety*. The child with partial sight is more vulnerable to every-day hazards and the choice of toys has to reflect this. Play

objects that have sharp edges should be avoided, as should toys that are easily breakable and those that are small enough to be swallowed.

- *Easily cleaned.* All children go through a phase of exploring objects by putting them in their mouth. The child with a visual difficulty is likely to continue with this habit for longer than a sighted child, and so toys should be able to be cleaned without suffering damage.

Parents may have a choice of establishments for their child with visual difficulties when he reaches nursery age. Much depends on the local provision provided by the individual education authority. An ordinary nursery may be willing to admit a pre-schooler with visual impairment, as long as the staff are given some basic advice about the child's specific needs by his psychologist. Placements like that provide the child with the normal range of pre-school activities and give him the experience of mixing with other children of his own age. At first, the child may feel very timid and be lacking in confidence. But careful supervision and encouragement by nursery staff usually overcome this problem. The other children in the nursery are nearly always thoughtful and understanding.

In contrast, there are also specialist nurseries set up specifically to meet the needs of children with partial sight. This type of nursery is staffed by personnel specially trained, and specially interested, in the education and development of pre-school children with visual difficulties. Some parents prefer these special nurseries because they feel they offer the children more expert care, while others prefer ordinary nurseries because they feel they allow the children to have a more typical sort of life.

Whatever the eventual pre-school placement, the years at home leading up to it are very important. A stimulating and sensitive upbringing, that concentrates on the child's strengths and not on his visual weakness, is the best start to life that a child with partial sight can be given.

10 · Discipline

Discipline is an essential part of parenthood. Caring and sensitive discipline helps children because it provides a structure and consistency in their lives, and because it sets out clear standards of behaviour for them to follow. Another effect of discipline is that it encourages children to consider other people's feelings, as well as making them feel safe and secure.

Many parents of a child with special needs become over-protective, almost as if they feel firm discipline is bad. A study conducted in Scotland, comparing the way parents discipline their child who has special needs with the way they discipline their other children, found that 34 per cent of mothers and 43 per cent of fathers were less likely to punish their child with special needs when she broke family rules.

A similar study organized in Northern Ireland revealed that 53 per cent of parents were less rigorous in enforcing discipline with a child who had special needs, and 46 per cent were less likely to punish their child for minor transgressions. Many of those who did use punishment actually felt guilty about it. Closer observations of the parents who claimed they disciplined all their children in the same way, revealed almost 20 per cent were in fact more lenient with their child who has special needs.

One explanation for this reluctance is that the child's parents are reacting to feelings of guilt. By being 'soft' with the child, they are unconsciously expiating their own deep-rooted guilt. A more likely explanation, however, is that many parents believe their child with special needs is more vulnerable than an ordinary child, less able to withstand the pressures of everyday life, and consequently that she needs to be protected.

Although a child with special needs has developmental weaknesses, this is not a valid justification for over-protectiveness. You should remember that discipline helps your child's development; it has many positive aspects and is not just a system of rules for controlling her. Don't lose sight of this – it will reassure you of the purpose behind your actions. A child with special needs benefits as much from well-organized family discipline as any of her brothers and sisters.

WHEN DISCIPLINE SHOULD BEGIN

Psychologists disagree over when discipline should start. Some think a baby cannot be expected to follow rules because she is too young and immature to understand what is going on around her. These professionals firmly believe parents should respond to their baby whenever she cries. Others think that discipline should start at birth, and that the undisciplined baby will turn into an undisciplined child. These professionals believe that a rigorous feeding, sleeping and changing routine should be followed at all times.

There is no 'right' answer to this, although there is no point in disciplining a child who is too immature to understand what it is you are trying to achieve. Certainly a young baby can learn that crying is a good way of getting her parents' attention, and many parents find themselves becoming totally exhausted when they fall into the pattern of responding to their baby every time she cries. Yet failure to respond can also be detrimental to the baby's development. Consistent refusal to react positively to a crying baby teaches her that she is not very important. It communicates the message that although she is unhappy her parents are not going to do anything to relieve her distress. Repeated experiences like that will reduce her feelings of security, and she may cry more frequently as a result.

Another factor to consider is the baby's health. Some conditions responsible for developmental delay (particularly Down's Syndrome) may have associated medical problems, such as a heart murmur. Or the baby may have breathing and swallowing difficulties. In these circumstances, parents are likely to be reluctant to let their baby cry for any length of time, for fear that she may choke.

However, that fear may not be based on reality. It is essential that parents get clear medical advice on this from their child's paediatrician, before deciding how to respond to her crying.

All these factors should be weighed up, although it is worth remembering that every child needs consistency in her life. A balance should be struck between rushing to the baby every time she whimpers and ignoring her completely when she cries. If you do decide to ignore your baby when you hear her crying, make sure you look in on her regularly – without letting her see you, of course.

THE ATTENTION-SEEKING CHILD

Some babies and young children have the knack of pushing their parents to the absolute limit with their demands to be the star attraction, and are able to turn any situation to their own advantage. It is as if they have an intuitive knowledge of their parents' weak spots – like the baby who starts crying once again just as her mother thinks she has lulled her into sleep, or the child who has a screaming tantrum in the supermarket just as her mother reaches the check-out.

But that does not mean parents are unable to change the way their child behaves. Although, in most instances, psychologists are unable to explain why some children are more attention-seeking than others, they are able to state confidently that a child's minor desire for attention – which is only natural – will become more intense if the parents do not take appropriate action. The first step you have to take when trying to counter the demands of your attention-seeking child – whether a three-month-old baby with Down's Syndrome or three-year-old infant with cerebral palsy – is to understand what is happening with the child. And to do that properly you have to understand some elementary principles of learning theory, because there is an element of learning involved in her behaviour.

When a child is born there are certain actions she does automatically, by reflex. For example, a baby cries for her very first feed, even though she has no idea that crying will result in food coming to her. A toddler who falls over automatically puts her hands out to protect herself from the fall. These acts of behaviour occur instinctively without the child even realizing she is doing them.

Yet most things that children do have to be learned. An infant learns that the sight of a bottle coming towards her means she is about to be fed, and she may show her anticipation by moving her arms and legs excitedly. The young child learns that she should try to tidy her toys away because her father shows he is pleased, and the child likes this. She also learns not to touch fragile ornaments in the house, because that behaviour incurs a reprimand and she does not like this. A child with special needs may take longer to learn how to behave, but the underlying principles of learning are always the same:

- *If something your child regards as positive immediately follows one of her actions, then there is a high probability that she will repeat that same action in the future.* The link between her behaviour and the favourable result reinforces the child's desire to do it again.
- *If something your child regards as negative immediately follows one of her actions, then there is a lower probability that she will repeat that same action in the future.* The link between her behaviour and the unfavourable result diminishes the child's desire to do it again.

This seems simple enough. And if that is all there was to bringing up children then parents would have an easy time of it. However, there is another principle of learning in children:

- *A child may like a certain event even though her parents do not.* It is not always easy to appreciate exactly what it is that a child enjoys. Many babies and young children would rather have any form of adult attention in preference to any type of material object. So although the parents think that a smack on the bottom will discourage their child from misbehaving, that reprimand for a disruptive action actually may be attractive from a child's point of view. After all, negative attention is better than no attention at all. There are situations where a parental rebuke actually encourages the very behaviour that it is intended to eliminate. For example, even though the child's father may be furious with her when he is told by playgroup leaders that she pushes the other children out of the way to get the toy she wants, the expression of that fury means the child is getting her father's full attention.

CONSISTENT MANAGEMENT

The application of these theoretical principles about the way a child learns behaviour leads to practical suggestions for dealing effectively with the attention-seeking child:

- *Give her what she wants – that is, attention – but give it at varying times for different actions.* You have to control when the child is given attention. If you only attend to your child when she is being naughty, then she will learn to be naughty every time she wants attention. So be prepared to give your child attention, spontaneously, when she is not expecting it. Play with your baby when she is settled and contented. Praise your child when she is being well-behaved. Your unexpected cuddle can be sufficient to meet the child's emotional needs. It takes away the necessity to misbehave in order to get attention.
- *Try to ignore negative attention-seeking behaviour.* There are may occasions when punishment seems to have no discouraging effect whatsoever, except perhaps to encourage the child to carry on misbehaving. Ignoring the undesirable behaviour can be very effective – but it is difficult. Requiring your strong resolve, a solid refusal to respond to the child's negative attention-seeking behaviour can discourage it.

Both these principles have to be applied consistently – especially with a child who has special needs because her rate of learning may be slower – if they are to have an impact on your child's behaviour. You will not see much change in your baby's rate of crying if you ignore her for, say, thirty seconds, then turn round and scream at her. Similarly, there is no point in making a special effort one day to praise the child because she is behaving well, then letting two weeks lapse before you do the same again. You have to be consistent in what you do.

That principle of consistency applies to all aspects of discipline for your child with special needs. Everybody requires some structure and stability in life. Although there are times when your household rules should be flexible, in most cases if parental limits have been set, your child should be expected to follow them. Inconsistency confuses a child.

ADMINISTERING DISCIPLINE

You have to decide for yourself what style of discipline you feel most comfortable with. Although every family is unique, you may find the following suggestions helpful for your child with special needs.

Present rules to your child in a caring and sensitive way. She is much more likely to respond to your demands if she feels that you are establishing discipline because you love her than if she thinks you have rules because you cannot be bothered with her. A child with special needs is as sensitive as any other child. And explain to your child the purpose of each rule. Keep explanations very basic and use terms that she can understand, for instance, that taking her friend's toy away without asking will make her friend cry. And emphasize that she will benefit from rules just as much as anyone else. For instance, the rule that children do not punch each other means she will not be hit by another child.

Be prepared to take action if your child regularly breaks the rules. If you have made it clear to your child that she will be punished in a specific way for breaking a specific rule, then stick to what you have said. Empty threats simply teach a child that her mother and father do not mean what they say. Special needs or not, your child will soon be able to assess how far she can push you.

Punishments should be realistic and meaningful to your child. The most effective form of punishment is one that the child regards negatively, not necessarily the one you regard negatively. But don't smack her. That will only make her more disruptive, more aggressive, and less amenable to your discipline. Find a more suitable punishment, something you know she does not like, such as being put out of the room for five minutes, or not being allowed to watch her favourite video that night. Short and precise punishments are the most effective.

The timing of any punishment has a direct influence on its effectiveness. The use of rewards and punishments to reinforce your discipline has an optimum impact on the child's behaviour if they are given immediately after the behaviour has occurred. This is particularly important when dealing with a child who has special needs, because her short-term memory may be limited – too long a delay in administering the punishment may mean that she does not see the connection between it and her misdemeanour. The longer the time between your child's actions and your own response, then the less effective is your discipline.

Punishments should be counterbalanced by rewards to encourage your child to behave well. Praise your child when she acts appropriately. There is no harm in giving a child a special treat as a reward for having a particularly good day. That will encourage her to follow rules in the future. She needs this incentive from you.

Your child may be very demanding and may deliberately misbehave throughout the day. In that situation, you could find that you are being challenged constantly by her. And that has to change. You should aim to establish more appropriate behaviour, while trying to avoid conflicts with your child over matters where you cannot win. There are some areas of behaviour that you cannot control unless your child cooperates fully with you, for instance, feeding, sleeping or using the toilet. No parents can force their child to eat food that is in front of her, to go to sleep when she is told to do so, or to empty her bladder and bowels on demand. So do not use these aspects of behaviour as testing grounds for your discipline.

SPOILING A CHILD

Parental reluctance to discipline a child with special needs can result in a spoiled child who is over-indulged, strong-willed and determined to get her own way every time no matter what anyone else wants. A spoiled child exercises control over her parents (not the other way round as is usually the case in parent–child relationships) and is uncooperative when things don't go her way. This type of child is rarely happy because she always wants more than she has already got. And she will not be popular because she will be unable to take turns in a game, or to let others choose the play activities, or to share her toys. This causes unnecessary problems for a child with special needs when she has the opportunity to mix with other children.

Few parents deliberately set out to encourage a child to have all these undesirable qualities. Instead, spoiling seems to be one of those processes that creep up on parents without them noticing, until someone else points it out. By then, however, the pattern of spoiling is well established, and the child will strongly resist any parental attempt to change the situation. That means that a spoiled young child will develop into a spoiled older child.

So maintain a reasonable and consistent family discipline. And avoid falling into the trap of showering your child with an over-abundance of presents, or she will soon expect to get something every time you take her out shopping with you. Make sure there are some occasions when your child does not get what she wants. Even if your child has an ample amount of toys, clothes and presents, see to it that she does not get everything she asks for. That teaches her how to cope with situations that do not go the way she wants. The relative balance between when a child gets what she wants and when she does not get what she wants, is more important than the absolute amount of things that she gets.

Even though you may not want to spoil your child, you may find these wishes being undermined by the child's grandparents, who think that she deserves this 'special treatment' because of her developmental problems. Many people regard presents as being synonymous with love, and so grandparents often reason that the more presents they give, then the more they must love the child. Put your foot down if you want to discourage this – you are the child's parent, they are not.

11· Expectations and Achievements

Childhood is characterized by two conflicting trends. On the one hand, a child is dependent on his parents for love and security, and this emotional connection with his parents gives him a strong psychological foundation for later life. On the other hand, a child also develops his natural tendencies to be independent.

Independence – being able to do things without help from anyone – covers many aspects of development, including having bladder and bowel control, being able to eat using cutlery and to drink out of an open cup without spilling any of its contents, being able to put on socks and shoes, and being able to ask for something. In fact, independence covers all aspects of a child's life.

A child with special needs, however, will have difficulty establishing independence in some areas (for example, spina bifida may delay his starting to walk, a communication difficulty may inhibit his ability to ask questions) and he will need more encouragement (because everything may be such an effort for him). But every child is capable of advancing his development in some way. Your support is crucial to his establishing independence.

KNOWLEDGE OF DEVELOPMENT

Knowledge of age-related stages of independence is important. The Developmental Checklist given in Appendix I indicates what children at each age are normally able to do. Yet that knowledge by itself will not give you clear guidance on how to encourage your child to be more independent. It is more important for you to know the orderly sequence in which these skills are acquired because you will not be able to help your child advance unless you are aware of the stages of development lying in between your child's level and the desired level. So when studying the checklist for each skill, try to become familiar with the sequence through which your child is expected to progress – that way you will know what his next stage should be.

There are specific teaching programmes for use by parents at home with their children, which provide this sort of information. The *Portage Guide to Early Education*, a popular programme designed specifically for parents wanting to teach skills to their own child with special needs at home, is a guide to the behaviours most children learn during the time from birth to six years of age. The behaviours are listed in the order in which they are usually learned. Whelan and Speake's *Learning to Cope* also provides a well-organized, stage-by-stage teaching scheme to encourage the development of pre-school children with special needs.

Some parents reject this type of approach on the grounds that it is too clinical, that it over-formalizes what should be a natural aspect of the parent–child relationship. These parents prefer to have an approach that they feel is individually designed for the particular needs of their child, rather than using a prepared skills-improvement package. It comes down to personal preference, and you should only interact with your child in a way that you are all comfortable with.

PARENTAL ATTITUDES

Have realistic expectations of your child. If you expect too little of him, he will not realize his full potential – and if you expect too much of him, he will give up without trying. Your task is to present a challenge to him that is just ahead of his current level, but not so far ahead that he feels there is little point in trying to attain it.

Some parents allow their child to progress at his own pace in the belief that because he has developmental problems then he should not be 'pushed' too quickly. Other parents demand too much of their child with special needs. One study found that parents of a group of children with a speech defect had unrealistically high expectations of their child's future progress, while another study found the same applied to a group of mothers of children with cerebral palsy.

Psychologists have looked at this issue more closely, and have revealed an interesting paradox. Results of a project in which parents were involved in detailed discussions of developmentally-delayed children, showed that most of them had an accurate view of their child's present level of development (concurrent realism). However, many of the parents predicted long-term advances in their child's development (predictive realism), which were way ahead of those predicted by professionals. This mismatch between concurrent and predictive realism can ultimately be a cause of anxiety for parents.

ENCOURAGING INDEPENDENCE

Training your child to be independent can be tiresome because of the demands it makes on you. But the following principles will give your independence training a clear structure:

- *Observe your child closely*. You need to know his present level of independence before you can move forward. Although he may not be able to turn a door handle completely, he may be able to go up to the door and touch the handle. Being able to do these smaller actions means he is part of the way there already, and you can set your goals accordingly. You also need to observe your child in order to assess progress.
- *Decide what you want your child to achieve*. Goals have to be very specific so that you know precisely what to aim for. 'Putting one arm through the sleeve in his jumper, during dressing' is a clearer goal to aim for with your child than 'managing his clothes on his own'. Specific aims like that are easier to achieve than are vague ideas.
- *Avoid being over-protective*. The only way your child's independence will increase is through experiences that challenge him. If you shelter him too much, he will remain dependent on you longer than is really necessary. So think about your expectations of him and make sure you are not being too protective.

- *Tell your child what each aim is*. Let your child know what it is you want him to achieve. Even if you are trying to teach a skill to a toddler, talk to him as you interact with him. If he does understand what you are saying, then both of you will have a clear idea of what has to be done. It also means that with certain tasks, such as putting on his socks, he can practise when you are not with him. If he does not understand what you are saying, talking to him will still make the experience more enjoyable for him.

- *Improve independence in gradual stages*. Slow and small steps towards independence are easier to achieve than huge jumps. This is extremely important for children with special needs. Break down each task into lots of small, easily attainable stages, and then work through these in the correct sequence. When trying to teach your child to drink out of a cup on his own without spilling it, make the first stage that he should lift the cup to his mouth, even if he does not drink from it. Then aim for him to touch the cup to his lips. Then aim for one or two drops to go into his mouth, and so on.

- *Give your child feedback on his progress*. Tell your child how well he is doing on the task. Feedback like that is crucial in all learning situations. A child with special needs may benefit more from it because he may not be able to assess his own progress accurately – you may have to highlight it for him.

- *Love and praise*. Independence training can be stressful for the child, especially when he experiences failure along the way. Give him lots of praise when he does become more competent at each task, and reassure him that he will be able to do it eventually. Your encouragement is crucial.

- *Don't rush your child*. Give him plenty of time to achieve the specific task. A child desperately trying to dress himself in the morning before going out to playgroup can be highly inconvenient for the rest of the family who want to get out of the house in time for school or work. You will be tempted to dress him, for the sake of speed, but that only works against independence. Make sure you leave the child enough time to complete the task. The conditions need to be relaxed and supportive, not hurried.

- *Keep practising skills the child has already acquired*. He should continue to rehearse things he can already do. This may be boring for him, but research has demonstrated that this repeated practice (over-learning) is a very effective way of ensuring the child retains the skill.

- *Don't overdo it.* You may be tempted to keep going continuously when encouraging your child to be more independent, especially if he is achieving success. But that may exhaust everyone's patience and interest. At any rate, bear in mind that five minutes spent learning a skill, followed by a fifty-minute break, followed by a further five minutes learning the same skill, can be more effective than if the child had been learning the skill without a break for the entire hour. Sensible breaks are essential. 'Teaching sessions' with a child who has special needs should last no more than five to ten minutes, even though he may be thoroughly enjoying the activity.

TOILET-TRAINING

Bowel and bladder control is one of a child's major achievements on the road to independence. Parents vary in their attitudes towards this. Some believe that toilet-training with their child who has special needs should be started as soon as possible because that will encourage him to be more like other children of his age. Others believe that the child will learn 'in his own good time'. And in many instances, the older the child is before toilet-training begins, then the quicker success is achieved. This happens because the child has to have reached a certain stage of physical maturity – he needs to be able to control his bladder muscles – before full control is acquired, and the older the child, the more likely it is that he has reached that stage.

Toilet-training should begin only when your child shows readiness, which is signified by his awareness that he is passing urine or having a bowel motion. He will indicate this awareness by communicating to you (using words or gestures) either that his nappy is wet, or when he is actually wetting his nappy, or that he is about to wet his nappy. Where the child does not indicate any such awareness, another sign that he is ready to begin toilet-training is when his nappy is dry even though it has been worn for several hours. Most children learn bladder control after bowel control.

There are some children with special needs who will never learn toilet control because of their associated physical difficulties. A condition affecting the spine (such as spina bifida) may render the child permanently incontinent. Or a child may have a medical problem with his bladder. But this is less common than many parents assume, and so you should seek medical advice before concluding that your child's lack of bladder and bowel control is a medical, rather than a learning, difficulty.

The guidelines given earlier in this chapter for encouraging independence also apply to toilet-training, but in addition the following suggestions specifically about toilet-training may be helpful.

Even before you begin training, let your child play with a potty, and let him sit on it with his nappy on. This way he becomes used to the sight of the potty and to its name. After this initial phase, gradually explain to him what the potty is for, and keep it beside the toilet bowl in the bathroom. Let him go to the toilet along with his brothers and sisters, or with you – as long as neither you nor they are embarrassed by the presence of a curious toddler. Your child will want to be able to do what the others in his family can do, so the opportunity to watch his older brothers and sisters in the toilet will encourage him to imitate them.

Once your child is showing signs that he is ready for toilet-training, pick times during the day when you sit him on the potty. Since you want the child to achieve success wherever possible, make sure the times you select for training are times when you think he usually wets or soils his nappy. The best times are usually after mealtimes or snack-times.

Have the potty handy, within easy reach of the child, so that he can get to it as soon as he feels the need. Many parents toilet-train their child letting him move around the house without any nappy on during the day. This is an effective strategy as long as he has instant access to the potty. As well as that, dress him in simple clothing. There is no point trying to establish bladder control if it is a struggle to undress your child from the waist down. During toilet-training, make sure his nappy or training pants are easily accessible.

Try to stay calm, no matter what response your child makes. He may think it is all a big joke, and he may decide to get up and wander about the room. As luck will have it, you can be sure that a couple of seconds after he moves away from the potty he will empty his bladder all over the carpet. Try to keep your temper during these occasions. Remind him that he should use the potty and that you will try again later in the day. Do not let it become an area of conflict between you.

Give your child regular and frequent opportunities to toilet. That will enable him to establish some sense of routine. And allow him to sit on the potty whether he is toileting or not. There is no harm in letting your child look at a book while on the potty, or listen to music. If these measures help him feel at ease, then all to the good (although you should remind him why he is sitting there). But avoid leaving him sitting on the potty for too long – ten minutes at a time is probably enough.

Never physically force your child to sit on the potty if he is reluctant, no matter how frustrated you may be feeling because of his lack of cooperation. You are bigger than him so you will have the required strength to detain him there. But you cannot force him to empty his bladder or bowels on command. Pressurize him like that and the chances are that he will dirty the floor the instant he leaves contact with the potty. Toilet-training has to be done by negotiation and persuasion, not bullying.

When your child uses the potty properly – whether by intention or by good fortune – give him lots of praise, and reward him in whatever way you feel is appropriate. Tell him why you are so pleased, and that soon he may not have to wear a nappy at all.

Lastly, keep things in perspective. Don't expect toilet-training to go smoothly, and be prepared for your carpet to get wet and dirty. Never punish your child simply because he does not fill the potty at the most convenient moment for you. That will reduce his self-confidence, increase the tension between you, and decrease the speed of his learning process.

Children become dry at night after they become dry during the day. The most common sign of readiness for night training is when you find that his night nappy is regularly dry in the morning when he wakes up. Boys frequently take longer than girls to become dry at night. Common-sense rules apply to night training. Make sure the child toilets before going to sleep, check that he can reach the toilet at night if he wakes up (leaving a light on in the toilet all night if necessary), or keep the potty close to his bed if that is more convenient. Do not give him lots of drinks before he goes to sleep.

There is no scientific evidence that a child who wets at night is a very deep sleeper. A child can pass urine at any stage in his sleep, not always at the deepest moment, and most commonly when he is moving from a phase of deep sleep into lighter sleep. Some parents lift their sleeping child when they themselves are going to bed and take him to the toilet. Yet this can be counter-productive because it involves the parents taking the responsibility of toilet-training away from their child, on to themselves. Nor is there any evidence that depriving a child of drinks in the evening will help him become dry at night. Of course, the child should not be plied with glasses of juice prior to bedtime. But even total deprivation will not stop his bladder filling during the night.

A child who starts to wet at night after he has been dry consistently for a long period may be suffering from an infection or other illness, and this possibility should be investigated by the family doctor. However, it is more likely that the wetting is due to an emotional difficulty. Many parents mistakenly underestimate the emotional sensitivity of their child with special needs. But the fact that a child has special needs does not mean he is less susceptible to emotional stress. Like any other child, he has sad moments and happy moments, and moments when he is anxious about something. So losing bladder control temporarily at night can be a sign your child is under stress. Seek professional advice if the problem persists.

UNTYING THE APRON STRINGS

Many parents start to get their child used to short separations even when he is a baby, by encouraging him to spend a few moments in someone else's arms, by leaving him in the care of a friend or relative for a few minutes, or by having him sleep in a separate room as soon as he comes home from the maternity hospital. When he is older, his parents might deliberately encourage him to spend a few hours at a friend's house, or they might leave him in the care of a child minder. Early experience of short separations from parents – separations not due to ill-health or trauma – can be part of independence training and help lay the foundations for later self-sufficiency.

The first major separation from you in the young child's life is the start at playgroup or nursery – and you should encourage your child with special needs to attend such a pre-school provision. Perhaps for the first time, your child is away from you, having to cope without you holding his hand. A distressed reaction to the start at playgroup or nursery is commonplace. However, you can take positive steps to help your child through this phase:

- *Talk to staff at the playgroup or nursery well in advance.* Inform the staff of your child's developmental problems, his strengths as well as his weaknesses. That way you will feel confident about leaving him there. The information will also increase the staff's confidence in managing your child. Make sure the professionals involved with your child – for instance, the psychologist, health visitor and medical officer – discuss your child's special needs with the staff at the playgroup or nursery.

- *Prepare your child for the event by talking to him about it beforehand.* Do this well before he is due to start, and visit the playgroup or nursery with him beforehand in order to familiarize him with the adults there and the building. Your child may not have the maturity to understand exactly what you are saying, but he will probably realize the main point you are trying to make.

- *Be calm and relaxed when taking the child there each day.* You will probably feel anxious, particularly on the first day, because the start at nursery is the end of one chapter in his life. But do not show any signs of your own concern. If your child does appear to be worried, reassure him that there is nothing for him to be concerned about.

- *Set yourself a timetable for leaving.* While you will probably stay with your child all the time during the first few days at playgroup or nursery, you should then start to leave him there for increasingly longer periods. For example, after a few sessions of your being with him the entire morning in the playgroup or nursery, leave the building for ten minutes and then return. The next day, increase your time away to twenty minutes. Continue this, each day gradually extending the amount of time you are away from your child.

- *Be resolute, determined to see your plan of action through.* Your child has to be absolutely certain that the separation will take place whether he wants it or not, and that his tears will not change anything. If you are inconsistent about leaving him, then you may find that his separation difficulties continue indefinitely.

- *Once you have established a pattern of separation, do not linger at the playgroup or nursery once you have arrived there.* Leave promptly each time, even though there are occasions when he appears upset at your impending departure. (The most usual time for that to happen is after weekends, or after holiday periods.) Hand the child over to one of the staff so that he has someone to look after him.

- *Talk about the day's events when you collect him at the end of the session.* That will encourage his interest in the nursery activities, by focusing attention on it. The more he sees you are interested in what happens there, then the more likely it is that he will develop a positive attitude towards it.

12 · Play

Play is important for every child, because it is through play that a child learns about herself and her world. Play allows a child to explore the environment, to test out what lies in front of her. It also allows her to get to know herself and her own abilities. With an older child, play provides an opportunity to interact with other children, and to develop her creativity and imagination. All these varied forms of learning occur through the medium of play. And the marvellous aspect of it all, as far as the child is concerned, is that play is fun.

Curiosity is usually the driving force behind a child's desire to play with an object. The determination to get to know what a rattle is all about spurs the young baby into action. She will stretch out, straining for it if necessary, until she has the rattle in her hands. The baby will even cry in frustration if she cannot reach the object that she wants to play with.

A child with special needs, however, may not appear to have that apparently natural curiosity. She may have no desire to explore her immediate surroundings. A baby with special needs may be quite happy to lie in her cot all day without trying to strike the mobile hanging above her, or without trying to get a sound from the activity centre attached to the side of the cot. An older child with special needs may prefer to sit watching television all day, resisting any attempt by her parents to engage her in a more dynamic activity.

But that does not mean that the child cannot play. It simply means that she may require more encouragement than other children of her age to get involved in play activities. There can be several reasons for this. First, she may have physical difficulties which interfere with her ability to touch, handle and manipulate toys. A child with cerebral palsy, for instance, may be unable to make her hands go in the direction she wants. That factor can quickly reduce a child's interest in exploratory play. Second, she may have learning difficulties which reduce her ability to see the relationship between her actions and their consequences. An infant with delayed development may not realize that it was her hand movement which was responsible for the musical toy making a noise. Third, the toys she is offered may not be appropriate to her needs. Some toys for young children are the all-or-nothing type, in that the child experiences either success or failure. A shape-sorter comes into that category – the child either can put the right shape in the right hole at any given moment, or she cannot. When a child realizes she cannot master that item, then she will soon lose interest. Other toys allow a child success no matter what she does. For instance, there is no 'right' way for an infant to play with a ball. She can hit it, throw it, roll or even lick it – and so it is appropriate for any age.

Roy McConkey, a leading British psychologist, totally rejects the idea that children with special needs cannot play. His theory – one shared by most professionals – is that play can enhance the learning skills of children with special needs. McConkey acknowledges that a child with special needs may not be able to play in the same way as other children her age, either because she plays immaturely or because she uses the toy inappropriately. But that does not mean the child is unable to play.

McConkey's view rests on a close examination of research studies into the development of play in children with special needs. One of the first investigations into this topic was published in 1942. The researchers observed twenty-five children with special needs aged eleven years, and twenty-five children with satisfactory development aged seven years. (The researchers had judged both groups to be at a similar stage of development.) Some differences in play between the two groups emerged from these detailed observations. For instance, the children with special needs chose very structured toys (jigsaws, card games, etc.) whereas the other group preferred more creative open-ended activities (drawing, building bricks, etc.). More significantly, however, the researchers found that although a child with special needs may require some prompting to start her play, once she has begun she is likely to spend as much time on it as any other child would. Other studies of children with particular developmental difficulties, such as cerebral palsy, partial hearing and partial sight, confirm that virtually all children with special needs do play.

TYPES OF PLAY

There are many different types of play, each stimulating the development of a different aspect of a child's life. The particular form of play that a child engages in at any one time will depend on her level of maturity, her individual interests and the toys she has available. Each category of play is not mutually exclusive, and any one play sequence can have more than one purpose (throwing her plate on the floor might result from her curiosity to see the pattern made by the food when it hits the carpet, or it might result from her desire to see if she is strong enough to push the plate off her table). But being able to identify the different types of play may help you understand the motivation underlying your child's actions.

Exploratory/discovery play allows a child to investigate objects, to find out what they are like. A child can smell an object, or touch it, or feel its texture, or perhaps even put it in her mouth so that she can taste it. Only by reaching out and exploring her immediate world in this way does a baby begin to make sense of her surroundings. Exploratory play can often be self-perpetuating. The more a child makes discoveries about the characteristics of objects, the more she wants to explore even further. And along the way, this discovery process helps the child develop her exploratory skills, such as reaching, grasping, hitting, pulling, shaking, turning, all of which will help her tackle new learning situations. The child with special needs often requires extra encouragement to explore in this way, perhaps because her coordination is not well developed, or because she takes longer to master new skills.

Physical/energetic play takes place once a child is able to move around independently. This is a more adventurous type of play because it involves her moving her entire body, unlike exploratory play which might only involve the child's fingers and hands. Physical play – whether crawling, running, jumping, balancing, climbing or kicking – requires the child to do things for herself. And that is a great boost to the child's self-confidence and independence. Physical play is especially important for a child with special needs because she may have problems with balance and coordination which can be helped by this activity. The more control a child gains over her body movements through play, then the more she will be able to generalize this control to other aspects of movement, such as walking.

Creative play and imaginative play are often regarded as two separate kinds of play because the former involves the child making something (model, picture, puppet, etc.) out of materials, while the latter involves the child acting out a scenario. The point common to both these activities, however, is the opportunity they provide for the child to release her inner feelings in a way that is acceptable to adults. What is permissible in these fantasy worlds may not be permissible in the real world. A child would be severely reprimanded by her parents if she shouted angrily at them and told them to shut up – but that won't happen when the child pretend-plays that same scene with her friends acting as the father and mother. Likewise, a child would be punished for slapping someone in the face, but she will probably be given encouragement to squash and pummel a piece of modelling clay into shape. It is that freedom to express inner feelings – feelings which the child may not even know she is expressing – that makes both imaginative and creative play so important for a child's development. A child with special needs may have a high level of frustration because of the difficulties she has to cope with every day. And therefore these expressive media are even more crucial for her.

Cooperative play, the last stage in the development of social play, occurs when two or more children play together. Through these interactions, children learn how to get on with each other, to take turns, to follow basic rules, and to be fair with one another. Cooperation with others involves being able to take the other person's point of view, and therefore social play tends to make children less self-centred, more sensitive towards the other child. In some cases, social play will also involve arguments because one player is not behaving in the way that another player wants him to. The ensuing bickering – though hopefully it is not a permanent feature of a child's play – has value because the child will learn about herself and about the other child. This type of activity is as meaningful for a child with special needs as it is for any child.

The earliest stage of social play is known as solitary play because at this level a child is content to play on her own. She has no desire to be in the company of other children, let alone play with them. The child may even move away when other children approach. This is followed by parallel play, in which two children play in the presence of one another, although they do not actually interact. Each might watch the other, imitate the other and perhaps reach out and take the other's toy. But their private worlds of play do not connect. As a child matures, cooperative play comes to the fore.

For many children, social play experiences occur many times in the day, perhaps when they meet a friend on the way to school, when they are standing in the playground before school starts, when they are walking along the school corridor or when they have friends over to play after school. Yet a child with special needs may not find social play so accessible nor so easy to engage in. She has a number of disadvantages in this respect. First, her more restricted lifestyle means that she does not have so many opportunities for that type of interaction, which in turn may mean she has difficulties getting on with other children when she does have the chance to mix with them. Then there is also the possibility that other children will reject her because she looks and acts differently from them. And lastly, if the child comes from a family that has responded to her special needs by spoiling her, then she will be used to getting her on way and will have difficulty accepting situations in which she does not come first.

The last major category is manipulative/cognitive/problem-solving play, in which a child learns by solving a puzzle. Completing jigsaws or building bricks to a particular pattern are examples of this type of play. Problem-solving play encourages a child to think about her actions, to plan them, and to learn through trial-and-error. A child with special needs may require extra help and encouragement from her parents when challenged by problems in play.

In understanding these different types of play, and the varied benefits they each bring a child, do not assume that a child can only be engaged in one type of play at a time. Any single action can serve several purposes. Throwing a ball to another child is social play because it involves cooperation, it is physical and manipulative because the child's hands and limbs are involved, and it could also be imaginative, if the ball becomes an entirely different object in the child's mind. Try to ensure, however, that your child has play experiences which seem to cover the whole spectrum.

GUIDING YOUR CHILD THROUGH PLAY

Your child probably requires your help to develop her interest and skills in play. The nature of her difficulties could mean that the sort of play situations you are familiar with are inappropriate to her. That is why some parents of children with special needs prefer a prepared, organized programme for directing play in the house. There are such schemes available. Dorothy Jeffree and Roy McConkey's *Let Me Play* is a highly structured programme of games aimed at promoting motor and sensory skills, thinking skills, imagination and social confidence in children with special needs. Activities are specified in sequential order for each type of play. The *Portage Guide to Early Education* is another planned course of involvement. It is frequently used by home visiting teachers to teach parents how to set learning objectives for their children with special needs.

These schemes do not suit every parent. Some reject this approach on the grounds that it over-formalizes what should be a natural aspect of the child's life, and of the parent–child relationship. By structuring play too much, there is the danger that it becomes routinized and perfunctory. There is also the potential hazard that fulfilment of the programme assumes greater importance than the child's pleasure in each individual activity. Parents who take that view should adopt a more spontaneous approach to encouraging their child's play. But whatever way you plan to promote your child's interests in the many and varied forms of play activity, the following guidelines may be helpful.

Accept that your child may need a bit of 'prodding' to get her going. An infant with special needs in the very early stages of development may lie passively in her cot, observing the world as it revolves around her, without showing any desire to become actively involved. Or she may sit inactive in her chair. While that may be frustrating for you, it has to be tackled – and encouragingly, it is a problem which you will probably be able to overcome in time. If your child will not reach out for toys, then take the toys to her. Put the rattle in her hands, and even shake her hand for her so that she hears the noise it makes. Put her hands on a soft ball and gently squeeze her fingers round it. Actions like that stimulate the child's interest because she achieves success, and also sees how the toys can be used. In addition, you are providing an appropriate model of behaviour for her to imitate. A small amount of 'pushing' in the early stages can have a long-term positive effect on your child's play.

Match play activities to the level of your child's development, not the level normally expected of a child that age. There is no point at all in giving her a toy sold as being appropriate for children of her chronological age if she is not mature enough to play with it. Study her toys and the way she plays with them. That way you will know her current level of development, and be able to give her suitable toys.

As with all learning situations with a child who has special needs, progress should be made in small, finely graded stages. The critical aspect in harnessing a child's curiosity is to make the activity sufficiently advanced so that she is interested in it, but at the same time not so advanced that she finds it overwhelming. A child who just manages to fit the pieces of a three-piece form-board into their correct places will have little enthusiasm for a six-piece jigsaw, but she will probably enjoy tackling a four-piece form-board. And a child who is unsteady on her feet may balk at the prospect of negotiating a climbing frame, but she may enjoy standing on a step. You have to observe your child's play closely over a few play sessions, to determine her current level, before setting a new activity for her. That will be time well spent.

By all means, encourage your child to expand her skills and

interests. But ensure that you do not push at too hard a pace. The best motivation to progress is success, and your child is most likely to try new items when they are in a graded sequence of difficulty. That will increase her self-confidence and her willingness to continue. Let her play at the same level for some time before suggesting to her that she moves on to something more challenging.

Play along with your child, as long as you both feel comfortable in that situation. A child who is lacking interest in a play activity will become more enthusiastic if she sees her parent playing at it as well – and if she is already playing, your involvement will encourage her to persist. Remember, though, that it is the child's play session, not yours. Avoid dominating and being too directive.

Never let your child see your disappointment or anxiety at her lack of progress in a game, puzzle or physical activity. Much as you may feel disheartened at what you perceive to be a lack of progress in your child's development, make sure she does not know you feel that way. She herself is probably disappointed at her lack of success. Play should always be fun – when play becomes an area of tension, your child will avoid it.

Show your child how to solve a particular item if you think she has been persisting in vain for too long and is beginning to become distressed by her lack of success. Demonstrating to her how to do it does not necessarily diminish her chances of learning from the activity, especially if afterwards you ask her to show you how she can do it. This sequence of demonstration followed by practice can be a very effective form of learning through play.

There is a wide range of special toys for children with special needs. This has been a growth industry in the past decade, although many of the toys are made by specialist manufactures. Advances in electronics mean that flashing lights, buzzers or music can be added on to a toy in such a way that they are only triggered when the child manipulates the toy in a particular fashion. The electronic response acts as a reward for the child's appropriate play. Many children with special needs respond positively to this range of equipment. The National Toy Libraries Association (see Appendix III) is able to give parents the address of local toy libraries with special toys for lending. Local specialist support services for children with special needs should be able to advise you too. There is also a wide range of computer software for children with special needs.

Give your child plenty of opportunities to play, both by herself and with other children. Since your child may have fewer opportunities for social play, make a specific point of inviting other children over to your house for her to play with. And do not be afraid to supervise her in social play if you feel she is not as mature as her playmates. She may need to be taught how to take turns, or how to cope with losing at a game. Role-playing these scenarios with your child before she interacts with other children will help her cope more adequately with the real situation when it arises. (This is discussed in more detail in Chapter 5.)

13 · Integration and Education

Once the early years of childhood have passed, the next major issue all parents have to tackle is that of their child's schooling. And the central dilemma is whether his special educational, social and emotional needs can best be met through being integrated into the local primary school, or in a segregated special school (a school staffed by specially trained teachers, with small classes, specialized equipment, and attended only by pupils who have special educational needs).

Although integration (known as 'mainstreaming' in the USA) of children with special needs has been given major backing in the 1980s and 1990 by educationists, it is not a new concept. For instance, as early as 1955, Circular No. 300 from the Scottish Education Department stated that 'special educational treatment should, indeed, be regarded as a well defined arrangement within the ordinary educational system to provide for the handicapped child the individual attention that he particularly needs'.

Some ordinary schools, particularly those in small rural communities, have integrated pupils with special needs long before the current drive to make this more widespread. In an inner-city school, such pupils may well attend segregated special schools. However, the very close-knit community in which the rural school operates frequently precludes segregated provision. The school is seen as an integral part of the community and consequently there is often a greater acceptance of individual differences.

A turning-point in attitudes towards integration arose in America in 1971. PARC (Pennsylvania Association for Retarded Children) instituted a case in the Federal District Court arguing that children with special needs were being denied access to a free public education. The Court declared that the state was not entitled to operate such a discriminatory educational policy. A similar federal decree was declared in the District of Columbia a year later.

These court decisions, coupled with the continued efforts of pressure groups (especially the American Civil Rights movement), resulted in the US Act of 1975 (Public Law 94-142) which states that children with special needs (note that the term 'handicapped' is still used at this time) 'be to the maximum extent appropriate educated with children who are not handicapped ... and that special classes, separate schooling or other removal of handicapped children from the regular educational environment occurs only when the nature or severity of the handicap is such that education in regular classes with the use of supplementary aids and services cannot be achieved satisfactorily'.

In Britain, the Warnock Report (Special Educational Needs), published in 1978, emphasized the need for integration and expressed 'determined opposition to the notion of treating handicapped and non-handicapped children as forming two distinct groups, for whom separate provision has to be made'. This report formed the basis of the 1981 Education Act (England and Wales) which specifies that 'where a local education authority arranges special educational provision for a child ... it shall be the duty of the authority ... to secure that he is educated in an ordinary school', subject to the conditions that 'educating the child in an ordinary school is compatible with (a) his receiving the special educational provision that he requires; (b) the provision of efficient instruction for the children with whom he will be educated; and (c) the efficient use of resources'. (The Warnock Report and the subsequent legislation governing children with special educational needs is discussed in detail in the next chapter.)

Integration is not an all-or-none phenomenon. Instead, it develops along a continuum. And it does not happen simply because a child with special needs is placed in an ordinary school – he may, for instance, be rejected by his classmates, and be unable to cope with his individual curriculum. The Warnock Report identifies three levels of integration.

First, there is *locational integration*. This occurs when a special class – solely for children with special needs – is located within the building of an ordinary school, but where there is also very little contact between the pupils in the special class and the rest of the school population. Some parents are satisfied with this type of provision because it means that their child attends his local school, albeit in a restricted way. And it also means that the child is at the same school as his brothers and sisters. Other parents, however, reject locational integration on the grounds that it is no better than segregated schooling. Most people regard this level of provision as a stepping-stone towards more complete forms of integration.

Second, there is *social integration*. This occurs when a special class – again, solely for children with special needs – is located on the campus of an ordinary school, but where there are planned and deliberate opportunities for all the pupils to mix with each other at play times, meal times, and perhaps assembly times. These occasions allow unrestricted social interaction. Most parents of children with special needs regard social integration as a purposeful aspect of their child's schooling.

Lastly, there is *functional integration*. This is the fullest level of integration and occurs when pupils with special needs are not only located in the ordinary school and not only mix with other pupils at break times, but are also in the same classes. In other words, pupils with special needs are taught in the ordinary classroom – with additional help and resources as appropriate – alongside the other pupils of the school. Functional integration means the pupil with special needs participates fully in school life, just as much as anyone else. As such, parents and professionals usually regard this point on the continuum of integration as being the most conducive to the child's overall development.

The level of integration that is eventually achieved with individual children depends on a number of factors. For instance, the type of developmental difficulty experienced by the child plays a part. A child who is confined to a wheelchair may find locational integration a problem (perhaps because the layout of the school building greatly restricts the areas he can actually move to). Yet that same pupil might be functionally integrated because he has no learning difficulties and is able to cope with the normal curriculum along with all the other pupils. Similarly, a child with learning difficulties may be socially integrated and yet not be functionally integrated, because he requires a very specialized curriculum, even though he has adequate social skills.

The number of pupils with special needs in the ordinary school can affect the level of integration. If there are many children with special needs in any one school, there may be a tendency for them to socialize only with each other at break-times. That reduces their social integration. And a high number of pupils with special needs in any one class may strain the teacher's time (by requiring additional instruction in the class, extra help going to the toilet, etc.) to such an extent that adequate attention cannot be paid to each child's curricular needs. That could reduce the level of functional integration. However, this potential difficulty might be overcome with the help of an auxiliary member of staff in the classroom, since that would free the teacher from many routine non-educational tasks, giving her more time to work directly with the pupils. The teacher could also involve the other pupils in helping the children with special needs.

WHY INTEGRATION AND NOT SEGREGATION?

The justification for segregated special schooling for children with special needs primarily lies in the assumption that these schools can provide everything the child requires under one roof. All possible resources – including non-educational support, like physiotherapy and speech therapy – can be located in the one building, ensuring the child has constant access to all sources of help. The pupil does not have to take a day off school to visit specialists at health centres or child clinics. And segregated special schools have small classes (often with as few as eight pupils in each), usually with a specially trained teacher who can provide each child with an individualized educational programme. Segregated special schools also have an accumulated wealth of expertise in dealing with pupils with special needs.

Yet there has been an increasing awareness that segregated

special schools do not *per se* benefit the pupils who attend them. There is evidence that the pupils are disadvantaged educationally and socially. Children at segregated special schools do not necessarily receive greater educational gains than children with special needs who attend their local primary school. In 1988, a British research team led by psychologist Wendy Casey studied the progress of thirty-six children with Down's Syndrome, half of whom attended ordinary schools and half of whom attended segregated special schools for children with moderate learning difficulties. The children were assessed over a two-year period, with regard to their progress in expressive language, numeracy, verbal fluency and comprehension. Results showed that the pupils with special needs in ordinary schools made significantly greater progress in many of these measures (and compared favourably in all the other measures) than those pupils who attended segregated special schools.

Findings such as these have led some professionals to argue that there is, in fact, nothing 'special' about special schools. Some have even gone so far as to argue that segregated special schools are not there for the benefit of the pupils, but to reduce the pressure on teachers in ordinary schools.

Segregated special schooling also rests on the assumption that the pupil's social development will be best served by his mixing with other pupils at the same level of development. But there are disadvantages to this strategy. Peer-group relationships, aside from having a social value, also influence the child's learning skills and educational attainments.

American educational psychologist David Johnson argues that experience with a broad range of peers should not be thought of as a luxury for the minority of pupils, but as a necessary condition for every pupil to maximize his potential. Peer-group relationships provide a vehicle in which a child can learn attitudes, values and information not normally available from adults (for instance, aspects of sexual matters). Through his peer group, a child is able to test out his ideas, without being reprimanded by his parents for even suggesting the idea in the first place. These interactions also help a child cope with social relationships in later life – a very isolated child will experience social difficulties in adulthood.

Peer-group relationships enable the child to learn social skills necessary to function independently in society (for instance, how to get on with others, ways of asserting himself, listening to other people's points of view). They also allow the child to act out anger and aggression in a social setting, without any fear of retribution or punishment from adults. Peers tend to be more tolerant than adults of idiosyncracies of behaviour.

Another benefit of mixing with other children of the same age is that these interactions consolidate the child's sex-role identity. Although the development of gender awareness originates in parent–child relationships, this process is extended and enhanced by contact with other children of the child's own age. Similarly this type of contact may influence a child's educational expectations. A child interacting with higher-achieving peers can be motivated towards better personal academic attainments.

Segregated special schooling denies many of these potential benefits to pupils. And as a child grows older, the ability to relate to others in a wide range of social settings (for instance, in clothes shops, at the post office, in supermarkets, on the bus, in leisure activities) assumes even greater importance. Many parents of children who have attended segregated special schools say at the end of their child's schooling that while they have been delighted with the care and professionalism of the school, they are deeply concerned about the child's inability to cope with post-school society.

Bear in mind that integration does have potential disadvantages for the child with special needs. Primarily, he may experience social rejection from the other children in his class, especially in the early stages of his school life. This may make him unhappy and resentful. And even where the child does not meet such peer-group barriers, he may find it stressful to be working on a curriculum that is vastly different from the others. He may regard that as a constant daily reminder of his differences. However, these hazards can usually be overcome through sensitive management by school staff.

INTEGRATION AFFECTS THE FAMILY

Integration of a child with special needs has advantages for his family. Parents and siblings are likely to have a more positive attitude towards him if they see that every day he is able to function in an ordinary environment outside the home. As a result, they may pay less attention to his weaknesses and more to his strengths. Integration also means that the parents assess their child's development using dimensions applicable to every other child; the child is not treated as 'special', to the same extent that he would be when attending segregated special school.

Parents of a child with special needs who is integrated into mainstream schooling are more likely to encourage after-school activities with others the same age as their own child. Integration usually also continues in the child's social life. The parents too have more opportunities to interact with a wider group of parents.

Integration can also have disadvantages for the child's family. The greatest potential problem is that the child's attendance at the local school may emphasize his weaknesses. For instance, parents may see that every other child is able to walk independently from the playground to the classroom, or that every child can settle down to work in the classroom without intensive help from the teacher. Rejection by other children and parents can be very hurtful. There is also the additional stress on the parents of making sure that their child receives all the additional resources he requires. Integration means that the parents may, for instance, have to spend a lot of additional time taking their child to several after-school clinics (speech therapy, physiotherapy, audiology).

Although a child with special needs is the key figure in integration, the fact is that integration also affects the other pupils in the class. Parents of a child with special needs in mainstream schooling may be confronted by other parents who are anxious that their children may imitate inappropriate and immature behaviour of the child with special needs, or that the class teacher will spend too much time with the child who has special needs and not enough time with the rest of the class.

Despite these concerns, however, integration can have a positive effect on all the children in the class. Most teachers in an ordinary school with pupils who have special needs report an increased level of pro-social, caring behaviour amongst the pupil population. It is as if the presence of a child with special needs – and the caring way in which he is treated by members of staff – heightens the other pupils' sensitivities. Some parents of the other children use the child with special needs as an example of determination to motivate their own children, and these parents may take a more optimistic outlook on their own difficulties.

In 1987, Donald Bailey completed a research project, sponsored by the US Department of Education, which looked at the expectations of families of children with special needs and of families of the other pupils both before and after a nine-month period of integration. The main finding to emerge was that all the parents looked positively on integration, and felt that integration was working well for all the children. Parents of the children with special needs stated that in their view their children were accepted by all the pupils and that they benefited from exposure to the normal school environment. Many of the anxieties that parents in both types of family had about integration prior to the start of the project had eased by the time it finished.

AN OVERVIEW

You have to evaluate the potential value of integration for your own child in the light of his individual characteristics, your own strengths and weaknesses, and the quality of the school. Of course, there is a small percentage of children with special needs which are so severe that they can only be met within segregated special school, but many could be integrated into their local school.

First, you should think long and hard before committing yourself one way or the other. Talk it over in detail with your partner, and with the professionals involved with your child, weighing up the pros-and-cons again and again until you feel satisfied that you have fully considered all the factors. And include in your discussions the possible effects that your child's schooling could have on yourself and your other children – ask them their opinion. (Some local educational authorities have a policy of integrating pre-school children with special needs in the local nurseries. That provides a useful opportunity to give the child and his family experience of integration before formal schooling begins.)

Second, remember that current legislation supports your child's right to be integrated in his local school (subject to the conditions that his attendance in the local school 'is compatible with (a) his receiving the special educational provision he requires (b) the provision of efficient instruction for the children with whom he will be educated; and (c) the efficient use of resources').

Third, organize plans as much in advance as possible. Talk to the professionals involved with your child, and ensure that they make all the necessary arrangements. Don't leave anything to chance. And meet with the teacher who will be teaching your child once he starts attending school. Express your concerns, and tell the teacher about the difficulties you anticipate your child may experience. But remember, also, to let the teacher know about your child's strong points, and any particular interests he has. That will give a more balanced view of your child.

Fourth, make a definite arrangement to have regular contact with your child's teacher. You should not be hovering on the school doorstep every minute of the day, but neither should you allow long-term problems to develop without your knowing about them. A short parent–teacher meeting each week, lasting perhaps five or ten minutes, is a useful plan, especially during your child's first term at school. And expect his progress to be reviewed at regular intervals, because his needs will change as he grows older. For instance, speech therapy may be less important at the age of ten years than it is at the age of five.

Finally, be prepared for 'teething troubles'. Most children find the start of school stressful – it is a whole new world for them, with different children and adults to relate to, different routines, and different challenges and expectations. So do not be surprised if your child has difficulties settling in. Expect the worst, and if all goes well, treat that as a bonus.

14 · Legislation

The education of children with special needs is governed by legislation. You should be aware of the relevant Acts, and the philosophy underlying them, because knowledge of your rights as a parent – and your child's rights to have an education appropriate to her special needs – will enable you to get the best for your child when she reaches school age.

The driving force behind the Education Act 1981 – the main piece of legislation regarding special education in England and Wales (there is a separate but similar Act covering special education in Scotland) – was the report of the Warnock Committee on Special Educational Needs (known as the Warnock Report), published in 1978.

The Warnock Committee had been established in 1974, following a proposal of Margaret Thatcher (then Secretary of State for Education and Science) the previous year, with the following terms of reference: 'To review educational provisions in England, Scotland and Wales for children and young people handicapped by disabilities of body or mind, taking account of the medical aspects of their needs, together with arrangements to prepare them for entry into employment; to consider the most effective use of resources for these purposes; and to make recommendations'.

The Committee's membership covered a broad spectrum of interests and expertise, and took into account almost 400 written submissions. The main body of the Report runs to over 360 pages, with more than 200 recommendations for action, including such diverse topics as the theory of education, curriculum, teacher training, parental involvement, school organization, identification and assessment, and relationships between professionals.

The most fundamental statement of the Warnock Report is the one which asserts that the goals of education, irrespective of the child's individual strengths and weaknesses, are 'first, to enlarge a child's knowledge, experience and imaginative understanding, and thus his awareness of moral values and capacity for enjoyment; and secondly, to enable him to enter the world after formal education is over as an active participant in society and a responsible contributor to it, capable of achieving as much independence as possible . . . the purpose of education for all children is the same; the goals are the same.'

The Report condemned the existing system of categorization which classified children according to their apparent disability (for example, physically handicapped, mentally handicapped, deaf, blind). That system was rejected because it 'promotes confusion between a child's disability and the form of special education he needs . . . Categorization perpetuates the sharp distinction between two groups of children – the handicapped and the non-handicapped – and it is this distinction which we are determined, as far as possible, to eliminate'.

The Report went on to suggest that approximately one in five children require some form of specialist help with their education at some stage during their school lives. Such specialist help should be flexible, should be adapted to the individual needs of each child, and should be subject to modification as the child's needs change throughout childhood. The Report recommended that special education should be thought of in terms of meeting the child's needs, and that there should be a formal system for recording children with long-term and significant learning difficulties.

Four main requirements of effective assessment of children with special needs were specified. First, there should be close parental involvement – no assessment is complete without the vital information that only parents can supply, and no educational programme can be implemented without parental support. Second, assessment should aim to identify how a child learns over a period of time, and not simply how she performs on a specific test on a specific occasion. The observations of teachers and others who know the child should also be included. Third, the assessment should focus on all aspects of the child's difficulties that are causing concern, and specialist views should be sought where required. And lastly, effective assessment has to take the family circumstances into account.

The Report developed this theme further, and prescribed five stages of assessment for children of school age, the first three stages informal and the next two stages formal. At stage one, the class teacher should have a discussion with the head teacher about a pupil who may have special educational needs. The head teacher is then responsible for gathering in all the relevant information – including medical and social information – about the pupil's school performance. Parents should be involved at this stage wherever possible. From this point on, the child's progress should be closely monitored, and detailed records should be kept. Stage two follows on from this and is the same as stage one, except that the head teacher should discuss the child's special educational needs with a teacher who is specially trained in special education. Again, the parents should be involved and kept informed of developments.

If the pupil fails to make sufficient progress, then the assessment should move on to stage three, when the head teacher would seek advice from a professional outside the school, for example, an educational psychologist, a peripatetic specialist teacher or a member of the health service. If it appears that the child's needs could be met within the resources of the school, then the assessment should not proceed to the next stage. The Warnock Report emphasized that these stages of school-based assessment should be flexible.

Stages four and five should involve multi-professional assessment. At stage four, the professionals involved should be those connected with local services, such as medical officers, educational psychologists, health visitors, social workers and learning support teachers. The professionals involved at stage five could be those involved at stage four, but there could also be professionals with a narrower specialism or responsibility for a broad geographical area. Assessment, therefore, should be a continuum moving from an informal school-based system to a more formal system which extends beyond the professional boundaries of the school.

An entire chapter of the Warnock Report is devoted to the theme of 'parents as partners', founded on the assumption that 'the successful education of children with special educational needs is dependent upon the full involvement of their parents; indeed, unless the parents are seen as equal partners in the educational process the purpose of our report will be frustrated'. Parental involvement was regarded as vital for the child's schooling to be effective.

That, then, is the model of good assessment practice, as recommended by the Warnock Committee. While such a system already existed in many local education authorities prior to the publication of the Warnock Report, there were instances which did not conform to this pattern. In particular, some parents complained that they were left out of the decision-making process and were not made aware of what was happening until the head teacher suggested that their child would be happier at a segregated special school. Other parents commented that specialist reports were sought without asking their permission, and that they were not told what the reports said about their child. Such practice, of course, was as unacceptable then as it is now.

THE EDUCATION ACT 1981

The main recommendations of the Warnock Report were translated into legislation in the Education Act 1981, along with the Education (Special Educational Needs) Regulations 1983, which came into force in April 1983. (In Scotland, the equivalent legislation is the Education (Scotland) Act 1981, and this is discussed in more detail later in this chapter.)

The Education Act 1981 abolishes the previous system of classifying children according to their handicap, and replaces this with the concept of 'special educational needs'. The Act states that 'a child has "special educational needs" if he has a learning difficulty which calls for special educational provision to be made for him' and explains that 'a child has a "learning difficulty" if (a) he has significantly greater difficulty in learning than the majority of children his age; or (b) he has a disability which either prevents or hinders him from making use of educational facilities of a kind generally provided in school, within the area of the local authority concerned, for children of his age'.

Under this Act, local education authorities now have a statutory duty for ensuring that 'special educational provision is made for pupils who have special educational needs'. In addition, the Act requires that local education authorities have first, to identify children with special educational needs, and second, to assess these children in order to determine the educational provision that will meet their needs. Parents have a legal right to ask the local education authority to assess their child, as long as the request is reasonable. (If the local authority decides not to carry out an assessment, the parents are able to appeal to the Secretary of State.) And whether the assessment has been initiated by the local authority or by the parents themselves, the parents have the right to be involved in the assessment process and to be able to submit their own views of their child's strengths and weaknesses.

The Department of Education and Science has issued instructions to local authorities, based directly on the Education Act 1981, about the assessment of children with special needs. Its Circular 1/83 (*Assessments and Statements of Special Educational Needs*) advises that assessment should follow the five stages outlined in the Warnock Report. The Circular also emphasizes to local education authorities that assessment of special educational needs is not an end in itself, but simply a vehicle for obtaining a clearer understanding of the child's difficulties. Assessment is a continuous process, which has to be on-going because children's needs change as they grow older. And you should bear this point in mind – your child's assessment will continue throughout her childhood, as long as she is of school age.

Whereas individual local education authorities are allowed flexibility over the manner in which the first three stages of the assessment are conducted, stages four and five are rigorously laid down in the Education Act 1981. To begin with, the Act specifies that if the local education authority proposes to assess a child's educational needs, then the authority must write to the parents explaining that an assessment is planned, how that assessment will be carried out, the name of someone in the local authority who can be contacted for further information, and the parents' right to submit evidence to the local authority within four weeks.

This notification, however, might be construed by an anxious parent as an insensitive, almost confrontational, approach. Couched in a formal style with legal jargon, a letter of this nature does not always instil parents with the feeling that the local authority cares about their child as an individual. (That is why many educational psychologists, who may be the coordinating officials for the local authority's assessment, do not post the letter to the parents. Instead, they may hand the letter personally to them so that they can explain the content there and then – this usually avoids any misunderstandings by the parents.) If you do receive such a letter without any accompanying explanation, make sure that someone from the local authority discusses the content of the letter with you face to face. You may find it helpful at that point to seek advice from a relevant voluntary agency (a list of useful organizations is given in Appendix III).

The local education authority is allowed to seek any advice whatsoever when assessing a child's special educational needs, but the Education (Special Educational Needs) Regulations 1983 specifies that it must consider a number of points when making its assessment, including direct representations from the parents (verbal or written), evidence submitted either by the parent or at the request of the parent, written educational, medical and psychological advice, and information relating to the health and welfare of the child from district health or social services authorities. Although local education authorities vary in the way this information is gathered, usually this is done either through the Education Department, or through the Schools Psychological Service (the Psychological Services, in Scotland), or through the combined efforts of these two departments.

THE STATEMENT

In England and Wales, the next stage in this part of the assessment is the preparation and compilation of a Statement of Special Educational Needs – a written account of the child's special educational needs and the measures that the local education authority intends to provide in order to meet these needs. (In Scotland, the equivalent document is known as a Record of Needs.) Neither the legislation nor the DES guidelines lay down the precise form of the Statement, and consequently the design may vary from one local authority to another. However, the content of the Statement is clearly defined in the Education Act 1981 and in the Special Needs Regulations 1983, and does not vary.

Every Statement is in five sections. Part 1 is an introductory page which sets out all the relevant factual details (name, address, age, name of parent or guardian, etc.) about the child who is the subject of the statement. Part 2 describes the child's special educational needs, as identified by those professionals who participated in the assessment. Part 3 specifies the educational provision that is considered necessary to meet the child's special educational needs. This part of the Statement would also specify any facilities, teaching arrangements, curriculum and equipment needed for the pupil. Part 4 indicates the type of school thought to be appropriate for the child, or the provision to be made if the child is to attend an establishment other than a school (for instance, a hospital). Where a particular school has already been selected (because the parents have already agreed it is appropriate), the name of the school should be included. Part 5 of the Statement contains details of any additional non-educational provision considered necessary to enable the child to benefit from the proposed special educational provision. This would be made available by a health authority, the social services or a similar agency.

The Statement is then signed by a representative of the local authority. The last part of the Statement – the Appendices – should indicate clearly all the evidence, advice, information and opinions taken into account by the local education authority when assessing the child's needs.

At this stage, the Statement is in draft form, and is sent to the parents, with an explanation of their rights of appeal. If the parents disagree with any of the contents of the Statement, whether on a major or a minor point, they have up to fifteen days to represent their views to the local education authority. This can be done in writing, although parents have a right to discuss their views face to face with a representative of the local authority. Should the matter not be resolved at that stage, the parents have a further fifteen days to ask for a meeting with the person whose advice they do not accept. The local authority has to comply with this request. Having heard the parental representations in this way, the local authority can either make the Statement in the form originally proposed, modify it, or make no Statement at all. The local authority must inform the parents in writing which of these options they intend to exercise.

Once the local authority has decided to issue the Statement, it has to send a copy of the final version to the parents. At the same time, the parents must be advised of their right to appeal, although it should be noted that they can only appeal against the special provision set out in Part 4 of the Statement. They cannot appeal against the local education authority's assessment of their child's needs. An appeal hearing – in front of an appeal committee consisting of members and non-members of the local authority – should be arranged well ahead of the due date, to be convenient for the parents. If the parents are not satisfied with the appeal committee's decision, they are able to make one last appeal, this time to the Secretary of State – and that minister's decision is binding on the parents and on the local education authority.

Confidentiality is crucial. Regulations confirm that in most circumstances no disclosure from the Statement can be made to anyone without the parents' consent. The exceptions to this are when disclosure is thought by the local authority to be in the child's educational interests, or when it is for the purpose of an appeal, or when it is for research (although even then, the child's anonymity must be preserved). The Statement must be fully available to the child's parents – it is usually kept in the main administrative offices of the local authority.

THE SCOTTISH SYSTEM

The basic principles of the Education Act 1981 are shared by the Education (Scotland) Act 1981, which covers special education in

Scotland. Both Acts are broadly similar in that they require the local authority to identify and assess children with special educational needs, and they both require a system of documentation. The role of parental consultation and involvement is paramount to both Acts.

In Scotland, the equivalent of the Statement for children with special educational needs is the Record of Needs. The exact format of a Record is specified in the relevant regulations. The front cover of the folder which holds the pages comprising the Record gives relevant factual information (name, address, age, etc.) about the child in question. Part II gives the parent's name and address. It also states who is the Named Person – someone appointed by the parents to act as a contact person to help the parents with advice and information. The Named Person can be an employee of the local authority, a psychologist, a doctor, a lawyer, or indeed anyone whom the parents feel confident of being able to help them discuss their child's education with the local authority. (In practice, many parents do not exercise this option, and elect not to have a Named Person.)

Part III of the Record of Needs sets out the child's assessment profile, which is a general description of the child's developmental strengths and weaknesses. It also has a section summarizing the child's impairments which result in her having special educational needs. Part IV is a description of the child's special educational needs, and divides these into 'sight, hearing and communication', 'intellectual/curricular', 'social/emotional' and 'physical/medical'. Part V of the Records of Needs is a statement of the measures proposed by the local authority to meet these needs, whether educational or otherwise (for example, speech therapy). Part VI details the school the child should attend, and Part VII is a summary of the parents' view (submitted previously in writing) about their child's needs. And Part VIII notes when the Record is reviewed and who has been allowed any information from it.

The Record is then sent in draft form to the parents for their consideration, similar to the system in England and Wales. There is also an appeal process. Where the parents appeal against the local education authority's decision to open a Record of Needs, the Secretary of State rules on this matter. Where the parents appeal against the specific school named for their child, the local Sheriff makes the final decision. (Some observers suggest this means the appeal hearing is more likely to be unbiased because the Sheriff is completely impartial.)

POINTS TO REMEMBER

The process for identifying and assessing a child who may have special educational needs follows a simple, well-defined and logical pattern. And if it unfolds in the way it is intended to, then the parents should be comfortable with the proceedings because they will be involved all along the way and they will know exactly what is going on at each stage of their child's assessment. Unfortunately, things do not always go according to plan. Some parents, sadly, have negative experiences of the system of assessment and recording, and are left with the feeling that the process serves the interests of the local authority rather than those of the child.

If your school-aged child is identified and assessed as having special educational needs, the following guidelines may help to reduce your potential anxieties and confusion:

- *Familiarize yourself with the legislation and regulations governing special educational needs.* You will not be able to ensure that the local authority is according you your rights unless you know what these rights are. So study this chapter closely. You may also want to obtain a copy of the Education Act 1981 from your local library.
- *Get involved from the start.* Discuss your child's difficulties with her class teacher as soon as you become aware that she has learning problems. It is very important that you establish a good working relationship with school staff, and the sooner this is started the better.
- *Listen to opinions.* Every parent is naturally protective – no one likes to hear apparently negative comments about their child. But you have to be prepared to hear what other people who know your child well, and who have worked with her in various learning and assessment situations, have to say about her strengths and weaknesses. Try to weigh up their comments objectively, without

rejecting them out of hand because you do not like what is being said to you.

- *Ask the professionals questions if you want further information.* Simply because a specialist (a psychologist, medical officer, speech therapist, physiotherapist, etc.) expresses an opinion about your child's learning difficulties, it does not mean this opinion is correct. You have to satisfy yourself that the specialist's opinion is based on a detailed knowledge of your child. And the only way you will be able to do that is by questioning the specialist concerned. Be wary if the specialist seems to resent your inquiries.

- *Make sure you are kept informed of developments as they arise.* You should be told when specialists are seeing your child and what work they are doing with her. If you find out that this information is not being passed to you, then voice your concerns, first to the people involved, and second, to your local education authority. Always put your comments in writing and keep a copy of it, and any subsequent correspondence.

- *State your own views.* The principle of parental involvement goes beyond having the child's parents at meetings. It also entails the parents being able to express their views about their own child, with the knowledge that these views will be treated with respect. So speak up, and say what you think.

- *Remember that the local authority, and its representatives, are working in the interests of your child.* Of course, there will be instances where officials and specialists are insensitive to the stress that parents are under when their child is being assessed. Yet the vast majority are not. Professionals want the assessment and recording to go smoothly. They know that unless they have your full backing, then the child – who is their client – will lose out.

- *Get in touch with the local authority official who has been designated as your contact during the assessment process.* Feel free to telephone or write to that person about any matter connected with your child's assessment. He is prepared to answer your questions, so do not feel you are being awkward by utilizing this facility.

- *Do not feel intimidated by the legal aspect of the assessment and recording process.* This can be offputting. The legalistic format of the letters accompanying the notice that the local authority is assessing your child, and the draft Statement (or Record), might almost seem abrasive. That is simply a reflection of the way the Acts are worded, not of the intention behind the Act. Seek clarification of anything you are unsure of.

- *Insist on seeing any provision that is suggested for your child.* On no account should you be expected – or should you agree – to pass an opinion on the suitability of a particular service or establishment for your child unless you have seen it for yourself. There is no justifiable objection to your wanting to visit a school recommended for your child, before you make up your mind as to its suitability. And if a particular service is suggested as necessary to meet your child's special educational needs (for instance, speech therapy or physiotherapy), talk to the specialist concerned about it before agreeing.

- *Ensure your child's progress in school is reviewed regularly.* This is a statutory requirement for children who have a Statement (or Record), but there is no harm in reminding the professionals involved that the time for a planned review is approaching. Assessment should be continuous throughout your child's schooling.

- *Try to relax.* Most parents are anxious about any assessment of their child. But remember that the assessment would not have been initiated unless your child was failing to thrive in her current educational placement. The successful intervention by professionals should mean that your child receives an education suited to her special needs, one in which her potential can be maximized.

Appendix 1
Developmental Checklist

As a parent, you will find the following brief checklist useful in gaining a deeper understanding of your child's progress. The checklist and the accompanying information in Chapter 1 will also give you an insight into the techniques and perspectives used by child psychologists when assessing the extent to which a child has special developmental needs. The checklist describes the milestones of development that children normally go through at each stage.

DEVELOPMENT AT THREE MONTHS

Gross motor development
- The baby has some head control at this age, whether lying on his back or face down. His head no longer flops about like a rag doll if not held securely by an adult who lifts him.
- The baby's vigorous kicking movements become more coordinated. Limbs move more in synchrony than they did before.
- Back firmness increases and the baby shows some signs of straightening his back when sitting on an adult's knee.

Visual-motor development
- He is now able to use his eyes to follow an object as it moves round the room. The baby can also follow a moving toy as it goes up and down, or from side to side, or even as it goes round in a circle.
- Being more alert, the baby will show an interest in any human face that happens to be in vicinity.
- The beginnings of hand control emerge. The child may suddenly bring his two hands together, almost as if he is not sure how he managed to do this.

Language development

- Although the child cannot move his head towards a sound-source, he may shift his eyes slowly from side to side, in search of it.
- Parents often report that at this age the child likes listening to music, whether on the radio or sung directly to him.
- The child is usually able to make at least two distinct sounds, such as 'goo' or 'la'. This is the start of language as a means of communication.

Social and emotional development

- The first smile will have been shown at around the sixth week, and this is the first indication of the baby's ability to derive amusement from his surroundings.
- Feeding becomes a tremendous source of emotional – as well as physical – nourishment. The three-month-old baby begins to focus on his parent's face during feeding.
- The baby enjoys company and familiar situations. He may smile when he realizes that bathtime has arrived.

Intellectual development

- An early sign of intellectual development is the baby's ability to see a link between his actions and a desired result. If a clean tissue is gently placed over a baby's face when he is lying on his back, he will make very general physical movements in a bold attempt to dislodge it.
- When a small toy is placed in his hand, his fingers will close round it at least for a couple of seconds.
- The baby at this age shows fascination with his hands. He will lock his fingers together, fan the air with them, or bring his hand up to his mouth to chew.

DEVELOPMENT AT SIX MONTHS

Gross motor development

- The child gains greater control over her limbs. When placed face down on the floor, she will be able to lift her head, shoulders and chest off the surface, pushing with her hands to help.
- When lying on her back, she will grasp adult hands as support to pull her head and shoulders up.
- By six months, most children are able to sit up on their own without any support, though they will occasionally topple over. When sitting up, the

child holds her head firmly and may even turn her head round if something catches her attention.

Visual-motor development
- The child is now able to keep her eyes on a toy that falls from her hands as long as the toy stays within her visual field. She will appear alert and interested, using her vision to explore her environment.
- She has better control over her finger movements. Rather than sticking rattles in her mouth as she did when she was younger, the child begins to use her toys more purposefully. She will shake them, rattle them or bang them deliberately in order to make a noise.
- The six-month-old child will watch an adult move slowly from one side of the room to the other.

Language development
- The child can now detect a sound-source more accurately, irrespective of which side the sound is coming from.
- She can usually produce at least four different babbling sounds, such as 'aa', 'goo' 'da' and so on.
- Speech becomes more closely linked to communication of feelings. The child may scream when she is annoyed or chuckle when she is playing happily.

Social and emotional development
- The child shows positive signs that she enjoys playing with a familiar adult, perhaps smiling or laughing occasionally.
- There may be the first signs of shyness in the presence of an unfamiliar adult, particularly if neither parent is with her.
- The child likes to keep any toy that she holds. If someone tries to remove it from her, even playfully, she may grip it even more tightly. Most small toys end up in the child's mouth, after she has passed them from one hand to the other.

Intellectual development
- The child uses physical movements more purposefully. Instead of trying to dislodge a paper tissue placed over her face by shaking her body, she will now simply pull it away.
- She is able to hold a small toy in each hand without dropping either of them.
- The child wants to get actively involved with her surroundings. When a

rattle is placed just outside the child's reach, instead of sitting and staring at it, she will reach out and grasp it.

DEVELOPMENT AT NINE MONTHS

Gross motor development
- The child can confidently sit up on his own on the floor, without any support, playing happily with the toys around him.
- Crawling is more coordinated. When a child is placed on the floor face down, with a desirable toy just out of his reach, he will make vigorous crawling movements in his attempts to reach it. Both knees are drawn and his arms might be stretched out, although he still cannot get the object.
- He may be able to stand up when gripping on to a low table or chair for support.

Visual-motor development
- When sitting in his pram, if the child accidentally – or deliberately – drops a toy, he will peer over in the appropriate direction, looking for it.
- If a small piece of biscuit is placed on his high-chair tray, the child will use his thumb and forefinger to bring it up to his mouth, rather like a pincer movement.
- The child is aware of the link between his hand and eye movements. He will pull a piece of string attached to a toy if he has been shown this by an adult.

Language development
- The child is able to use his hearing to pinpoint a sound-source accurately. He will immediately turn his head round when he hears his name.
- The infant will be using two-syllable babbles, for example, 'agah', 'eleh', regularly.
- The first word may appear at this age - it is usually 'mama' or 'dada'. The excited parental reaction on hearing this first 'real' word from the child acts as encouragement for him to say it again and again.

Social and emotional development
- The child can tell a stranger from a familiar person, and signs of shyness are obvious.

- Negative emotions can be expressed clearly. He will make a big fuss if someone takes his toy away while he is playing with it.
- During feeding, the child gets involved by trying to hold the spoon, or perhaps wrapping his hands round the drinking cup. Of course, he cannot yet manage these utensils on his own but he does make an effort.

Intellectual development

- If the child is holding one small toy in each hand and then he is given a third, he will probably drop one of the toys in order to accommodate the one being offered to him.
- He will have started to play with two toys together, for example, a plastic cup and saucer, or two small threading cubes.
- Children of this age love crumpling up paper.

DEVELOPMENT AT ONE YEAR

Gross motor development

- A child at one year is usually able to crawl around the floor on her hands and knees. However, some children prefer to 'bottom-shuffle' about the room instead.
- She is steadier on her legs and may be able to walk round furniture, for example a settee, by holding on to it firmly and side-stepping her way round.
- For many children – but not all – the early signs of independent walking are there. She may take some hesitant steps forward, holding on to an adult's hand for support.

Visual-motor development

- At one year, the child grips an object in a mature way, fully able to coordinate her thumb and forefinger in a pincer-type grip.
- Some children start to use a pencil or crayon properly by trying to make some mark on the paper instead of simply putting it in their mouth.
- There is great interest in every movement in the environment. A child of this age is fascinated by toys that roll across the floor in front of her.

Language development

- The child can use at least three clear words to describe familiar objects. And she uses these words appropriately, in the correct context.
- She will be able to follow basic directions. When asked to wave goodbye,

her correct response will confirm she understands what is required.
- The child will also talk away to herself when on her own or when engrossed in some play activity.

Social and emotional development
- At this age, social interaction interests the child. She enjoys playing very elementary games, such as pat-a-cake, with an older child or adult.
- She knows how to give – and receive – affectionate embraces to and from those adults she knows well.
- The child can hold a cup and drink out of it with only a little help.

Intellectual development
- Many children at this age can imitate adult actions. When shown how to bang two small wooden bricks together to make a loud noise, she will probably copy that action.
- While she is holding one brick in each hand, she will accept a third without dropping any.
- The child is fascinated by any object that rattles, and will want to know more about it. A couple of wooden beads rattling around in a small cardboard box will arouse her curiosity. This interest in simple puzzles is a positive sign of good intellectual development.

DEVELOPMENT AT FIFTEEN MONTHS

Gross motor development
- By this age, most children are tottering about – albeit rather shakily – on their own two feet.
- A child at this stage of development loves pushing wheeled toys about the house or in the street (under supervision). This activity boosts his self-confidence and feelings of independence.
- He may be able to kneel on his own on a chair while at the table, or perhaps on the floor while playing with toys.

Visual-motor development
- The child will have developed a preference for one hand over the other, and the grip in that hand is mature.
- By fifteen months, the child may be able to hold two small objects in each hand simultaneously – if only for a few seconds – before dropping them.

- A child of this age enjoys playing with moving objects. He will gleefully reach for a ball rolling towards him. If the toy is out of his reach and he cannot toddle about yet, then he is likely to point furiously at it.

Language development
- The infant likes rhymes and songs. He may try to join in singing, and familiar rhymes like 'Round and round the garden' or 'Knock on the door' will be greeted with delight, as he anticipates what comes next.
- The child can use at least three or four clear words in their correct context, and he will understand a lot more.
- Simple commands, such as 'Leave it alone' or 'Get your juice' should get an appropriate response from the child.

Social and emotional development
- The child is more cooperative, keen to help in his basic management. When getting dressed, he tries to help, perhaps by putting his arms out in anticipation, or getting his own slippers.
- This desire to get involved extends to feeding as well. The child should be able to use a spoon for feeding himself, although some of the contents may get spilled in the process. With help, he might be able to hold a cup and drink from it.
- Exploration is the name of the game at fifteen months. Constant supervision is needed as the child's enquiring mind takes him into all sorts of interesting – but possibly hazardous – parts of the house. Ordinary household items become transformed into toys as the child rattles, for example, a packet of dog biscuits to discover what sort of noise it makes.

Intellectual development
- Boxes of any size seem to have an inherent fascination for children of this age. At first he may just rattle a small box given to him, but eventually he will remove the lid and get the contents out. The more mature child will put the contents back in the box if requested.
- Elementary form-boards can be used at this age. Most good toy shops now sell form-boards with only one or two shapes in them. If the child is shown how the shapes fit in the board, then he may be able to do it by himself.

DEVELOPMENT AT EIGHTEEN MONTHS

Gross motor development
- At this stage, the child is usually able to walk comfortably and steadily on her own, and may even be able to trot about the room.
- The eighteen-month-old infant can bend down and pick up a toy from the floor, without losing her balance.
- Climbing ability has improved. The child should be able to climb into a low armchair, and then turn round and sit back. If the chair is small enough, she can slide backwards into it.

Visual-motor development
- The child will probably manage to build a tower of three building bricks before it falls over.
- Pencil control is more mature. The child can scribble freely on paper.
- Her interest in books is positive. She enjoys story-time and points out recognizable objects that appear in the pictures.

Language development
- Vocabulary is now at least six clear words, although the child understands many more. She tends to prattle on using long babbled sentences, with some of the words intelligible.
- When the eighteen-month-old infant wants something, whether it is a glass of milk, or the television turned on, she will point to it, using some form of language to indicate her wish.
- When spoken to, the child will listen to what is said. Even though she may not be able to say the word herself, she will carry out the instruction properly.

Social and emotional development
- The desire for independence shows through. The child makes good efforts to manage her own feeding. She can drink out of a cup without spilling much of the contents. The spoon consistently reaches her mouth, and very little falls on to the table in the process.
- Home becomes an environment to be explored. The toddler will make energetic attempts to open and shut doors. She can also take off her unfastened shoes and socks by herself.
- Despite this wish to do things on her own, a child at this stage of development can be very clingy to her mother and father at times.

Intellectual development
- Interest in form-boards continues. The child can cope with more complex puzzles of this sort, with perhaps three or four pieces in them.
- The child may be able to empty her toy bricks out of their box, then put them back in and fit the lid on securely.
- The child's memory is sufficiently mature for her to be able to remember where certain objects, such as her cup, or her favourite toy, should go. This means she can find them when she wants and – hopefully – is able to put them away when she is finished.

DEVELOPMENT AT TWENTY-ONE MONTHS

Gross motor development
- The child climbs up and down stairs without adult help.
- Motor skills are more advanced. He is steady on his feet and runs about comfortably without danger of falling over. The child may be able to jump from the floor so that both feet leave the ground at the same time.
- Some children at this age can walk upstairs independently. However, the child's lack of confidence may make him prefer to crawl upstairs on his hands and knees.

Visual-motor development
- The child will make a good attempt at throwing a small rubber ball. Instead of simply letting the ball drop from his hands, he uses his wrist in a definite throwing movement – although the ball does not always go in the desired direction.
- When playing with toy building blocks, the child can build a steady tower of up to five bricks.
- Improved pencil control allows the child to scribble in a more coordinated way. He will be able to scribble using long straight lines, rather than the haphazard strokes he used previously.

Language development
- Vocabulary is extended to at least twelve identifiable single words. And significantly, the child starts to combine them to form two-word phrases, such as 'Juice gone' or 'Daddy out'.
- He enjoys 'first picture' books which have one picture to a page, for example, a dog, a house, a table, etc. He will be able to name at least one of these objects accurately.

Social and emotional development
- The child begins to develop an understanding of body parts. When shown a doll, he can point to one or two items when asked, such as hair, eyes, feet, nose, and so on.
- Some children aged twenty-one months have bladder control, but this depends greatly on the parents' attitude to toilet-training. Many parents prefer to leave this to slightly later.
- The child shows signs of wanting to tell others about his daily experiences, and, although language is not well developed, he can communicate, for example, that he saw his favourite programme on television, or that his playmate took his toy away.

Intellectual development
- The child can complete unfamiliar form-boards without requiring much practice, as long as there are only three or four pieces to them.
- Memory continues to improve and he can reliably find familiar items in the house, without being told where they are.
- Many children of this age become engrossed in imitating whatever their parents are doing in the house. Previously, the child would only do this for a short time, but now involvement in this activity is sustained.

DEVELOPMENT AT TWO YEARS

Gross motor development
- Using a wall or bannister as support, the child walks up and downstairs on her own, though she still puts both feet on one step before moving up or down to the next.
- Being steady on her feet, the child can walk or run up to a ball and kick it without falling over.
- A child of this age enjoys sitting on a tricycle, or indeed on any pedal toy. Although she cannot use the pedals to propel the toy, she moves it along the floor by pushing with her feet.

Visual-motor development
- The child can now build a steady tower of at least six or seven blocks.
- Because her pencil grip is more mature – she holds the pencil towards the tip, using the thumb and first two fingers – the child can make a reasonable attempt to copy a vertical line.
- She is able to pick up very small objects with ease. The toddler will be able to unwrap a small sweet without difficulty.

Language development
- Vocabulary is at least twenty or thirty words, and the child understands a lot more. She talks in short sentences, putting two or more words together to make a meaningful phrase.
- The child listens to what is said to her and she attends to any general conversation that is going on around her. When playing on her own, the child often talks continuously to herself.
- When asked to identify certain body parts, the toddler can reliably indicate hair, eyes, nose, mouth and feet.

Social and emotional development
- The child can open and close doors by herself. However, she does not have full appreciation of routine hazards so parents have to be very careful when she goes out of their sight.
- Tantrums often emerge at this age (hence the description 'the terrible twos'). This arises out of the child's frustration when she cannot get what she wants. The child may appear very stubborn, determined and demanding, especially when her parents show momentary interest in another child.
- Toilet-training is usually well underway by the end of the second year, and many children are reliably dry during the day.

Intellectual development
- The child's increasing ability to solve new situations means she can cope with jigsaws and form-boards of greater complexity.
- By two years of age, the child is ready to play with doll's house furniture and doll's house people, using them appropriately.
- The child may also refer to herself by her proper name.

DEVELOPMENT AT TWO-AND-A-HALF YEARS

Gross motor development
- The child makes reasonable attempts at jumping. With both feet together, he can push himself off the ground.
- Stairs are no longer the obstacle they used to be. The child is confident and capable enough to walk upstairs and downstairs again without help. However, he will want to hold on to a rail or bannister for support.
- If he has a toy wheel-barrow, or any large movable toy like that, he will be able to steer it along the ground without bumping into too many objects along the way.

Visual-motor development
- Picture books interest the child of this age. He will take great delight in spotting the small details in the pictures and pointing them out to an adult beside him.
- Hand preference is firmly established by now. The child will hold a pencil confidently, probably gripping it with three or four fingers, but steadily enough to make a mark on a piece of paper.
- Bead-threading is an activity that will attract the child's attention. However, he will have great difficulty in threading a lace through the hole in the bead unless both the bead and the hole are large enough.

Language development
- Pronouns come into the child's vocabulary for the first time. Words like 'me', 'I' and 'him' become a feature of the child's speech.
- By now he has a wide range of words in his vocabulary. The child will probably be able to use well over 100 words in their proper context.
- Most children of this age are able to tell another child or adult their first name when asked.

Social and emotional development
- Although the child is probably fully toilet-trained during the day, he may struggle to pull his pants and trousers back up after using the toilet. He should be able to pull them down by himself.
- Feeding habits have become more composed. He may experiment with his food but in general he will make good attempts to eat tidily.
- The child does not join in full cooperative play yet. He enjoys being in the presence of other children but will tend to keep himself to himself for the moment. He is not keen to share his toys or possessions with anyone else.

Intellectual development
- When shown a photograph of himself, on his own, without his parents in the picture beside him, the child will probably recognize himself.
- He will make a good attempt at copying a straight line drawn across a blank piece of paper, although his line may be a little unsteady.
- When shown coins, the child of this age will probably be able to say that they are money. However, he will not be able to identify individual coins.

DEVELOPMENT AT THREE YEARS

Gross motor development
- The child will be able to walk upstairs, like an adult, putting one foot on one stair then the other foot on the next stair. Coming down, she still puts both feet on one stair before descending to the next one.
- She can stand on her tiptoes and at the same time she can walk several paces without upsetting her balance.
- Large play apparatus such as a slide, balancing log or swing, will interest her. Some of the toys will be beyond her but she wants to try anyway.

Visual-motor development
- At this age, using small wooden building bricks, the child can build a tower of at least eight bricks before it falls over.
- She will begin to grip scissors properly. If allowed to use a pair of child's scissors, with their specially shaped handles, she may be able to cut up pieces of paper.
- Pencil control is improving. She will make a recognizable attempt to copy a circle. Similarly, she will enjoy painting pictures as long as the paint brush is large enough for her to grip comfortably.

Language development
- The child talks confidently in three- or four-word sentences.
- The number of 'who', 'what', 'when', 'how' and 'why' questions increase as her thirst for knowledge of the world around her increases.
- Her language becomes more elaborate. Perhaps for the first time, the child begins to use adjectives in her conversation. At this age, she probably has only two or three descriptive words but she uses them properly.

Social and emotional development
- The child has greater control over the use of cutlery during mealtimes. She is able to use a spoon and a fork together to feed herself, without any help.
- Many children of this age have bowel and bladder control throughout the night as well as throughout the day.
- She can dress and undress herself as long as the fasteners are not too small or complicated. The child can possibly manage to undo large buttons, but she is unlikely to be able to fasten them.

Intellectual development
- She can cope with larger form-boards now, perhaps with up to seven or eight pieces in them. The child will also be able to manage a two- or three-piece jigsaw.
- At this age, the first signs of colour recognition emerge. The child will not, as yet, be unable to identify all the primary colours by name, but she will be able to match two items of the same colour, especially if they are red or yellow.
- When drawing a picture of 'mummy' or 'daddy', she may draw in the legs and arms, as well as the head.

DEVELOPMENT AT FOUR YEARS

Gross motor development
- He can use pedals properly to propel a pedal car or tricycle along the ground.
- The child enjoys energetic outdoor play. He will take great delight in trying to master climbing frames, balancing logs, trampolines and swings.
- The child enjoys participation in ball games. Kicking, catching and throwing skills are all more advanced at this age.

Visual-motor development
- Cutting is more mature. Now, when using scissors, the child can cut a sheet of paper into two relatively similar-sized pieces.
- The child's drawing of his parents is more identifiable and contains more details, such as eyes, hair, hands or mouth, than his drawings did when he was younger.
- He can pick up very small items, for example, a piece of thread or a pin, without much difficulty.

Language development
- He is able to give an accurate account of relatively recent experiences at home and nursery.
- Colour recognition is more firmly established. The child may be confident enough to identify two or three colours.
- The child begins to develop a sense of humour. However, sometimes he will laugh at a joke simply because he likes the sound of the words, not because he really understands what the joke is about.

Social and emotional development
- The child can dress and undress himself without help, apart from small buttons, buckles and zip fastenings.
- By this age, he has begun to play cooperatively with other children. He accepts the need to share and to take turns. The child can quickly lose his temper when playing but is less likely to storm off in a huff.
- He will be able to give the correct response to 'How old are you?' or 'What is your age?'

Intellectual development
- He can complete jigsaws with up to fifteen or twenty pieces in them, although he may require your encouragement if he finds them difficult.
- The child will have the first stages of counting. He may be able to recite the numbers up to ten, or even beyond.
- Basic comparisons are within the child's grasp at this age. He will probably be able to differentiate successfully between two objects when deciding which one is larger/smaller, heavier/lighter, taller/shorter, and so on.

DEVELOPMENT AT FIVE YEARS

Gross motor development
- The five-year-old is agile and able to engage competently in various physical activities such as running, jumping, climbing and kicking.
- She is totally independent on the stairs, going up and down without any help at all. The child is also able to run upstairs without falling over.
- Other physical skills, involving balance, should be well developed. The child can hop several paces on one foot, and she can skip from foot to foot.

Visual-motor development
- Some children at this age are able to make an identifiable attempt at writing one or two letters, usually the ones that appear in their names.
- Drawing skills are more mature now. Many children are able to draw a recognizable house, with windows and doors in it, and a recognizable man, with arms, legs and hands. Pencil or crayon control is better, allowing the child to colour in shapes more neatly than before, without straying over the outline.
- She should be able to copy some simple shapes without much difficulty.

Language development

- At this age, the child is able to speak quite clearly and has little difficulty in making herself understood by unfamiliar adults.
- She shows a keen interest in language and language activities, such as story-telling, nursery rhymes and songs, and even jokes. The child may also like singing advertising jingles that she has heard on the television or radio.
- Many five-year-old children are able to state their first name, their last name and their address, when asked.

Social and emotional development

- The child is able to eat properly using a knife and fork, assuming she has child-sized cutlery.
- Independence skills are well established. The child can usually dress and undress herself without help, can tidy away her toys and clothes when asked to do so, and can look after her basic cleanliness (as long as she is given regular reminders).
- Cooperative play is in evidence. She can mix well with other children, being able to participate in a game that has rules. Dressing-up play is very popular at this age.

Intellectual development

- The child is probably able to count up to seven, or beyond.
- She will have an idea about the different time phases of the average day, and will know that breakfast comes before lunch, that dinner comes at the end of the day, and so on.
- The child can match most colours and is able to name three or four colours confidently.

Appendix II
Suggested Reading

Adams, F. (1986) *Special Education*. Longman Group: Essex.

Bluma, S., Shearer, M., Frohman, A. and Hilliard, J. (1976) *Portage Guide to Early Education*. Cooperative Educational Service Agency: Wisconsin, USA.

Brennan, W. (1982) *Changing Special Education Now*. Open University Press: Milton Keynes.

Cunningham, C. and Sloper, P. (1978) *Helping Your Handicapped Baby*. Souvenir Press: London.

Curran, J. and Cratty, B. (1978) *Speech and Language Problems in Children*. Love Publishing Company: London.

Deitch, R. and Hodges, P. (1977) *Language Without Speech*. Souvenir Press: London.

DES Assessments and Statements of Special Educational Needs, Circular 1/83. DES: London.

Education Act 1981. HMSO: London.

Education (Scotland) Act 1981. SED: Edinburgh.

Education (Records of Needs) (Scotland) Regulations 1982. SED: Edinburgh.

Education (Modification of Enactments) (Scotland) Regulations 1982. SED: Edinburgh.

Education (Special Educational Needs) Regulations 1983. HMSO: London.

Evesham, F. (1989) *Help Your Child to Talk*. Cassell: London.

Galloway, D. (1985) *Schools, Pupils and Special Educational Needs*. Croom Helm: London.

Griffiths, M. and Russell, P. (1985) *Working Together with Handicapped Children*. Souvenir Press: London.

Jeffree, D. and McConkey, R. (1976) *Let Me Speak*. Souvenir Press: London.

Jeffree, D., McConkey, R. and Hewson, S. (1977) *Let Me Play*. Souvenir Press: London.

Kiernan, C., Jordan, R. and Saunders, C. (1978) *Starting Off: Establishing Play and Communication in the Handicapped Child*. Souvenir Press: London.

Lansdown, R. (1980) *More than Sympathy: The Everyday Needs of Sick and Handicapped Children and their Families*. Tavistock: London.

Marshall, M. (1982) *Parents and the Handicapped Child: A Guide for Families*. Macrae: London.

McConkey, R. (1985) 'Changing beliefs about play and handicapped children', *Early Child Development and Care*, 19, 79–94.

Meers, H. (1976) *Helping Our Children Talk*. Longmans: London.

Mitchell, D. (1982) *Your Child Is Different*. Unwin Paperbacks: London.

Pearson, L. and Lindsay, G. (1986) *Special Needs in the Primary School: Identification and Intervention*. NFER-Nelson: Windsor.

Philp, M. and Duckworth, D. (1982) *Children with Disabilities and their Families*. NFER-Nelson: Windsor.

Sutherland, A. (1981) *Disabled We Stand*. Souvenir Press: London.

Thomas, D. (1978) *The Social Psychology of Childhood Disability*. Methuen: London.

Warnock, M. (1978) *Special Educational Needs: Report of the Committee of Enquiry into the Education of Handicapped Children and Young People*. HMSO: London.

Whelan, E. and Speake, B. (1979) *Learning to Cope*. Souvenir Press: London.

Woolfson, R. (1989) *Understanding Your Child: A Parent's Guide to Child Psychology*. Faber and Faber: London.

Wyman, R. (1986) *Multiply Handicapped Children*. Souvenir Press: London.

Appendix III
Useful Addresses

There are many voluntary organizations throughout the United Kingdom, offering support and advice to parents of children with special needs. The main organizations are listed below, along with a brief description of their functions. You can contact them either by letter or by telephone. Inquiries from parents are welcome. National organizations, where applicable, will provide addresses of local groups.

ENGLAND

Association for All Speech Impaired Children (AFASIC)
347 Central Markets, Smithfield, London EC1A 9NH
Tel. 071-236 3632
Run for parents of children with specific speech and language disorders and for professionals, AFASIC provides information and advice for parents of pre-school and school-age children, and has regional support groups throughout Britain. The Association runs research projects, parents' conferences and has a full-time counsellor to discuss parents' anxieties with them.

Association for Spina Bifida and Hydrocephalus
ASBAH House, 42 Park Road, Peterborough PE1 2UQ
Tel. 0733 555988
Provides advisory and welfare services, practical assistance and information to parents and families who have children with spina bifida and/or hydrocephalus. The Association has its own team of trained fieldworkers and advisors. Study days are arranged for parents and professionals, and there is a training centre in Yorkshire.

British Dyslexia Association
98 London Road, Reading, Berkshire RG1 5AU
Tel. 0734 668271
Offers information, help and advice to parents of children with dyslexia/specific learning difficulties. A wide range of leaflets about specific learning difficulties is available. Specialist tutoring can be provided for pupils, through local associations. The Association also promotes the use of sound teaching methods for literacy, the early identification of children with specific learning difficulties, and research into all aspects of the condition.

British Epilepsy Association
National Information Centre, Anstey House,
40 Hanover Square, Leeds LS3 1BE
Tel. 0532 439393 for Head Office, though the Helpline is 0345 089599 and is charged at local rates
Advises parents on any problems – social, medical, educational – with their epileptic child. It also provides information packs to parents, and there are many local support groups. The Association's training officers are available to advise schools on the management of pupils with epilepsy.

British Institute of Learning Disabilities
Wolverhampton Road, Kidderminster, Worcs DY10 3PP
Tel. 0562 850251
Aims to contribute to an improving quality of life for children and adults with learning difficulties, and to encourage normal development as these individuals grow older. The Institute organizes workshops and conferences, publishes books and periodicals, provides an information and resource service, develops research, and encourages the coordination of services for those with learning difficulties.

Contact A Family
170 Tottenham Court Road, London W1P 0HA
Tel. 071–383 3555
Links parents of children with special needs into a network of over 700 self-help groups. Locally based groups usually cover a wide range of special needs, but 200 groups are run nationally for parents whose children have a specific or rare disorder. Contact A Family offers support and training to parents involved in running these groups, and operates an information, advice and linking service to the groups and individual families.

Cystic Fibrosis Trust
Alexandra House, 5 Blyth Road, Bromley, Kent BR1 3RS
Tel. 081-464 7211
Formed in 1964, the Trust aims to fund medical and scientific research
into cystic fibrosis, and has supported many projects in hospitals and
universities. All of Britain is covered by local branches of the Trust, whose
voluntary members help and advise parents about the problems associated
with cystic fibrosis.

Down's Syndrome Association
153–5 Mitcham Road, London SW17 9PG
Tel. 081-682 4001
Provides advice and information to parents with children who have Down's
Syndrome, and encourages parents to set up self-help groups nationwide.
It advises on a wide range of social, educational and health needs, providing
a link between parents and professionals. There is a London-based
resource centre which holds a wide range of literature, practical learning
aids, toys and audio-visual material, and which also acts as a meeting place
for parents and their families.

Dyslexia Institute
133 Gresham Road, Staines, Middx. TW18 2AJ
Tel. 0784 463935
The Institute was founded by parents, and now has seventeen major
centres and fifty teaching 'outposts' throughout the country. It provides an
assessment and identification service for dyslexics, offers specific teaching
help, trains specialist teachers and provides an information, advice and
counselling service for parents and teachers. The Institute also funds
research projects, and liaises with local educational authorities.

Family Fund
PO Box 50, York YO1 2ZX
Tel. 0904 621115
A government fund administered by the Joseph Rowntree Memorial Trust.
The Family Fund helps families with a child who has very severe developmental difficulties. The aim is to complement, rather than replace, existing
services in meeting certain special needs directly related to the child's
difficulties (such as laundry equipment, family holidays, outings, driving
lessons, clothing, bedding, recreational items).

Foundation for Conductive Education
University of Birmingham, Calthorpe House, 30 Hagley Road, Five Ways,
Edgbaston, Birmingham B16 8Q7
Tel. 021-456 5533
Recently formed for the sole purpose of bringing conductive education – a
controversial Hungarian treatment for cerebral palsy – to Britain. It has a
special agreement allowing it to provide conductive education in full col-
laboration with the Hungarian authorities, and is responsible for the Birmingham Institute for Conductive Education, which provides conductive
education for young children.

Handicapped Adventure Playground Association (HAPA)
Fulham Palace, Bishops Avenue, London SW6 6EA
Tel. 071-731 1435
Runs five adventure playgrounds in the London area for children and
young people with special needs. Its Information Service offers advice and
information to individuals and organizations interested in play for children
with special needs, and to other organizations wanting to establish similar
playgrounds in Britain.

Muscular Dystrophy Group
7–11 Prescott Place, London SW4 6BS
Tel. 071-720 8055
Main aim is to raise money for research into muscular dystrophy and the
allied neuromuscular diseases. The Group helps individuals and families
already affected by the disease, by providing practical help as well as advice
and counselling. It funds five Muscle Centres around the country, where
research scientists specializing in one aspect of neuromuscular disease
work alongside professionals providing support services.

National Autistic Society
276 Willesdon Lane, London NW2 5RB
Tel. 081-451 1114
This organization was established on the initiative of parents, in order to offer families advice and support, to provide literature on autism, to encourage research into autism, and to provide day and residential centres for children and adults with autism. There is an advisory and information service for parents and professionals on the nature of autism, the type of services available and teaching methods.

National Childcare Campaign
Wesley House, 4 Wild Court, London WC2B 4AU
Tel. 071-405 5617
Deals with all matters concerning young children, and campaigns for the integration of children with special needs into mainstream nurseries. It has no literature for parents, but acts as an information-base for parental inquiries and will put parents in touch with local contacts.

SENSE (National Deaf–Blind and Rubella Association)
Family Centre, 86 Cleveland Road, Ealing, London W13 0HE
Tel. 081-991 0513
Consists of families and professionals supporting deaf–blind children. The organization has a Family Advisory Service to offer help and advice from birth to all deaf–blind children and those caring for them, has information on welfare benefits, and organizes supervised holidays every summer for deaf–blind children and young adults. A series of books and information sheets is available. The regional and national offices seek to put parents in touch with other parents in their localities.

National Deaf Children's Society
45 Hereford Road, London W2 5AH
Tel. 071-229 9272
Working especially for deaf children, the Society provides information for parents, gives independent advice on education (including pre-school services and school placements), and provides welfare and holiday grants to families of deaf children. The Society also supports research into the integration of deaf children in mainstream schools, and runs courses for parents and professionals. It produces a wide range of publications, videos and children's books. Advice is given on hearing aids.

National Association of Toy & Leisure Libraries
68 Churchway, London NW1 1LT
Tel. 071-387 9592
Provides parents with addresses of local toy libraries, of which there are over 1,100 throughout the country. Many of these cater for children with special needs, by making special toys available through a toy-loan scheme, or by offering support services. Leaflets about play for children with particular difficulties are available for parents. Since toy libraries often work in conjunction with the statutory services, they may also be found in hospitals, health clinics and family centres. The National Association runs leisure libraries for young people who have been users of a toy library.

Prader-Willi Syndrome Association (UK)
30 Follett Drive, Abbots Langley, Herts WD5 0LP
Tel. 0923 674543
Founded in 1981, it is run by parents of children with Prader-Willi syndrome in conjunction with medical specialists. The Association provides support for parents and carers, and has information leaflets, handbooks, and medical texts all readily available. Medical research is actively promoted and funded. There are regional parent-support groups throughout the country.

Rathbone Society
1st Floor, Head Office, Excalibur Building, 77 Whitworth Street, Manchester M1 6EZ
Tel. 061-236 5358
Works on behalf of individuals with learning difficulties, with the primary intention of enhancing their lives. The Society offers support to families, develops youth training initiatives and employment opportunities, youth clubs, holiday schemes and play schemes and gives independent advice to parents. There is also a wide variety of publications available.

Royal National Institute for the Blind
224 Great Portland Street, London WIN 6AA
Tel. 071-388 1266
The Institute's Educational and Leisure Division helps children with visual impairment obtain access to the education facilities they need, by providing information pamphlets, advice and support for parents, teachers, and local authorities. Children's books in braille and on tape are available, as are specially adapted equipment and games. The Institute also advises parents on welfare benefits. There are parent-support groups throughout the country.

Royal Society for Mentally Handicapped Children and Adults (MENCAP)
123 Golden Lane, London EC1Y ORT
Tel. 071-454 0454
The largest national parent organization exclusively concerned with people with severe learning difficulties and their families. The Society provides support and help for parents through its divisional offices, district offices and a network of 550 local societies. MENCAP also runs residential services, training and employment services, and holidays. It offers staff training, legal and information services.

Spastics Society
12 Park Crescent, London WIN 4EQ
Tel. 071-636 5020
Founded in 1952 to alert the nation to the needs of people with cerebral palsy, it is now the leading organization in the world for education, training, care and other services for children and adults with the condition, and has established many schools, residential centres, industrial units, family help units and day care centres. The Society provides support and advice to parents of children with cerebral palsy.

Spinal Injuries Association
Newpoint House, 76 St James Lane, London N10 3DF
Tel. 081-444 2121
A self-help group for children and adults with spinal cord injury. The Association provides information on all aspects of living with spinal cord injury, and has a welfare service dealing with such matters as housing, benefits, sexuality and incontinence. The care-attendant service offers emergency and short-term help. The Association's holiday facilities include two specially designed boats controllable from a wheelchair, and

two caravans specially designed for a wheelchair user. SIA campaigns on issues affecting the everyday lives of disabled people. It runs a Personal Injury Claims Service.

Tuber Sclerosis Association
Little Barnsley Farm, Catshill, Bromsgrove, Worcs B61 0NQ
Tel. 0527 871898
Acts as a mutual support group for parents by sharing problems and giving information. The Association promotes a greater understanding of the problems associated with the condition, and undertakes fund-raising to finance research. It holds an international research symposium every three years. There is a benevolent fund for needy families.

SCOTLAND

Parental Help Evenings and Weekends (PHEW)
5 Bothwell Road, Uddingston, Glasgow G71 7EY
Tel. 0698 813482
Offers family-based respite care by receiving children with special needs into the homes of helping families, for weekends. The primary purpose is the relief provided for the children's carers. PHEW also runs its own respite care home, for individuals with severe and profound special needs, and offers stays of up to three days.

Scottish Council for Spastics
Rhuemore, 22 Corstorphine Road, Edinburgh EH12 6HP
Tel. 031-337 9876
Founded in 1946 to help children and adults with cerebral palsy achieve their goals, the Council provides education, care treatment and therapy to children and young people with cerebral palsy. It runs three schools, serving children from all over Scotland, has a mobile therapy unit, runs a residential home for adults, has two large industrial-training centres, and provides an extensive welfare service through its own specialist social workers. The Council develops sports and leisure activities for children with cerebral palsy.

Scottish Society for Autistic Children
24d Barony Street, Edinburgh EH3 6NY
Tel. 031-557 0474
Founded in 1968 by a group of parents, to meet the needs of Scottish autistic children. The Society runs Struan House School for twenty-four pupils, a young adult unit, and a community house for autistic adults.

Enable
6th Floor, Buchanan Street, Glasgow G1 3HL
Tel. 041-226 4541
A parent-based organization concerned with the needs and rights of children and adults with special needs, and aims to promote the welfare of these individuals. Through its local branches, the Society provides advice and support for parents, and runs two family-based respite care schemes for families. Activity holidays for children and adults are organized each summer. A Chair of Learning Difficulties at St Andrew's University was funded by the Society in 1986 to promote research and the better training of professional staff.

Scottish Spina Bifida Association
190 Queensferry Road, Edinburgh EH4 2BW
Tel. 031-332 0743
Assists families with a child who has spina bifida and/or hydrocephalus by acting as a channel for communication between parents and professionals, by disseminating information about the condition and its related difficulties, and by advising and assisting parents.

The following national voluntary organizations in the USA, Canada, Australia and New Zealand, should be contacted by parents and professionals to find addresses of local voluntary groups.

USA

Association for Children and Adults with Learning Disabilities
4156 Library Road, Pittsburgh, Pennsylvania 15234
Concerned with individuals who have specific learning disabilities (such as dyslexia). Offers advice on educational programmes. The Association has grown rapidly in the last fifteen years.

Association for Persons with Severe Handicaps
7010 Roosevelt Way, N.E. Seattle, Washington 98115
A multi-disciplinary organization to promote the interests of children and adults with major disabilities. It has a strong commitment to educational and community integration of people with severe learning difficulties.

Association for Retarded Citizens of the United States
National Headquarters, 2501 Avenue J. Arlington, Texas 76006
Formed by representatives of local and state parent groups to develop services and support for people with special needs. Its goal is full integration of the individuals into schools and the wider community.

Epilepsy Foundation of America
4351 Garden City Drive, Landover, Maryland 20785
Provides parents with advice regarding the care and development of children with epilepsy.

National Down's Syndrome Congress
1800 Dempster Street, Park Ridge, Illinois 60068–1146
Promotes greater opportunities for children and adults with Down's

Syndrome, and also aims to correct negative attitudes towards those with the condition.

United Cerebral Palsy
66 East 34th Street, New York NY10016
Provides advice and support to parents and relatives of children with cerebral palsy.

CANADA

Canadian Association for Community Living
Kinsmen Building, 4700 Keele Street, Downsview, Ontario M3J 1P3
A federation of ten provincial associations, concerned with the rights of children and adults with special needs. The Association deals with the government, and has a membership of parents and professionals.

AUSTRALIA

Australian Association of Toy Libraries for the Handicapped
c/o Noah's Ark Toy Library, 28 The Avenue, Windsor, Vic 3181
Formed in 1976, gives parents addresses of local toy libraries which offer services for children with special needs. Advises parents on appropriate toys for children with developmental difficulties.

Australian Council for the Rehabilitation of the Disabled
PO Box 60, Curtin, Act 2605
Conducts national consultations and lobbies on issues affecting all disabled people. It has committees on access and mobility, women's issues, recreation, health and medical aspects of rehabilitation.

National Council on Intellectual Ability
GOP Box 647, Canberra, Act 2601
Represents all state and territory voluntary organizations dealing with special needs. In addition to providing support and advice, the Council aims to promote better public understanding and endeavours to obtain recognition by the Commonwealth Government of intellectual disability as a major national problem.

NEW ZEALAND

New Zealand Society for the Intellectually Handicapped
National Office, PO Box 4155, Wellington
Formed in 1949, an umbrella organization for groups aimed at promoting the welfare and development of children and adults with special needs. Affiliated groups include the Down's Association, the Autistic Sub-Committee, Parent-to-Parent, and the Trust for Intellectually Handicapped People.

Index

The Epilepsy Reference Book
New Edition

JOLYON OXLEY and JAY SMITH

This is the main information source on epilepsy for patients, their families, GPs and other health workers. The diagnosis of epilepsy can have a devastating effect on people's lives. There is a desperate need for information on the subject. The new edition of this standard book covers all aspects of the condition. Details of diagnosis and medication are followed by information on the incidence and possible causes of epilepsy. Later chapters deal with long-term questions related to employment rights, travel, adjustment, diet, drugs, pregnancy, etc.

As well as helping patients to take more interest in their condition and form fruitful working partnerships with their doctors, the book provides information for the numerous other professionals – nurses, social workers, voluntary workers – who work with epileptic clients.

Faber Paperback   128pp
ISBN 0 571 16253 3   £7.99

ARE YOU A REGISTERED CHILDMINDER?
A WORKING PARENT?
OR INTERESTED IN CHILDCARE ISSUES?

The National Childminding Association is a membership organisation and registered charity which works to support Registered Childminders, parents and children. Registered Childminders are self-employed daycare providers who work in their own homes offering care and education for children, and more parents choose childminding than any other form of paid–for daycare.

The Association was formed eighteen years ago to promote childminding as a quality daycare service, to improve conditions for childminders, to encourage higher standards of daycare, and to keep childminders, parents, employers and central and local government informed about the best practice in childminding. We welcome new members - Registered Childminders, parents and other carers can all benefit from the services we have to offer.

What can the National Childminding Association do for you?

* We encourage childminders to join or set up local groups and can provide grants to help
* We lobby parliament and the media on behalf of childminders and parents
* We offer an information and advice service
* We produce a regular full-colour magazine, *Who Minds?* - full of information about childminding and childcare issues
* We offer public liability insurance for Registered Childminders
* We produce a full range of publications and leaflets to help childminders and parents

We're working for best quality childcare - why not join us!

For further details, send SAE to:
National Childminding Association
8 Masons Hill
Bromley
Kent
BR2 9EY